Blockchain

*A Beginner's Guide to Understanding the Technology behind Bitcoin &
Cryptocurrency and Learn How Blockchain is revolutionizing the
Financial World and How You Can Benefit from It*

Heinrich Brevis

Table of Contents

Introduction

Welcome to "Blockchain: A Beginner's Guide to Understanding the Technology behind Bitcoin & Cryptocurrency and Learn How Blockchain is Revolutionizing the Financial World and How You Can Benefit from It." This book is designed to demystify one of the most groundbreaking technologies of our time: blockchain. Whether you are a curious novice, an aspiring investor, or a seasoned professional looking to broaden your knowledge, this guide will provide you with a comprehensive understanding of blockchain technology and its implications.

Why Blockchain Matters

Blockchain is more than just a buzzword; it is a transformative technology reshaping industries and challenging traditional financial systems. Originally devised as the underlying technology for Bitcoin, blockchain has since evolved into a versatile platform with applications extending far beyond cryptocurrency. Its unique features—decentralization, transparency, immutability, and security—offer unprecedented opportunities for innovation and efficiency across various sectors.

The Rise of Cryptocurrency

At the heart of blockchain's popularity is cryptocurrency, a digital or virtual form of money that uses cryptography for security. The first and most well-known cryptocurrency, Bitcoin has sparked a financial revolution. Its success has paved the way for thousands of other cryptocurrencies, each with its unique use cases and potential. Understanding the mechanics of Bitcoin and other cryptocurrencies is essential for grasping the broader implications of blockchain technology.

A Financial Revolution

The financial world is undergoing a significant transformation due to blockchain technology. Traditional banking and financial services are being reimagined to leverage the benefits of blockchain, such as faster transaction times, lower costs, and enhanced security. From decentralized finance (DeFi) platforms to blockchain-based payment systems, the innovations are vast and varied, promising to make financial services more accessible and efficient.

How This Book Will Help You

This book is structured to take you on a journey from the basics of blockchain to its advanced applications and investment opportunities. Here's what you can expect:

- **Foundational Knowledge**: We will start with the fundamental concepts of blockchain technology, ensuring you understand its principles and how it works.
- **Cryptocurrency Insight**: You will learn about Bitcoin and other major cryptocurrencies, their histories, how they function, and their roles in the financial ecosystem.

- **Technical Mechanics**: We will delve into the technical aspects of blockchain, including decentralization, cryptographic hashing, consensus mechanisms, and smart contracts.
- **Broader Applications**: Beyond finance, blockchain is utilized in supply chain management, healthcare, digital identity verification, and more. We will explore these diverse applications and their potential to revolutionize various industries.
- **Investment Strategies**: For those interested in investing, we will provide guidance on navigating the cryptocurrency market, understanding different types of crypto assets, and developing long-term investment strategies.
- **Regulatory Landscape**: The book will also address the evolving regulatory environment, legal considerations, and compliance issues surrounding blockchain and cryptocurrency.
- **Personal and Professional Benefits**: Finally, we will discuss how you can leverage blockchain technology for personal finance, career advancement, and business innovation.

Embracing the Future

The world of blockchain and cryptocurrency is dynamic and rapidly evolving. Staying informed and adaptable is crucial. This book aims to equip you with the knowledge and insights needed to understand this complex yet fascinating field and help you recognize and seize its opportunities.

As we embark on this exploration of blockchain technology, remember that every great technological revolution began with curiosity and a willingness to learn. Whether you're looking to enhance your career, make informed investment decisions, or satisfy your intellectual curiosity, this guide will be your comprehensive companion in navigating the blockchain landscape.

Welcome to the future of technology and finance. Welcome to the world of blockchain.

Chapter 1: Introduction to Blockchain Technology

Imagine a world where banks, governments, or any centralized authority do not govern transactions. Picture a system where trust is not placed in institutions, but in the code that runs the network. Welcome to the world of blockchain technology, a revolutionary force that promises to reshape industries, economies, and our everyday lives.

The Genesis of Blockchain

Blockchain technology was born out of the chaos and mistrust of the 2008 financial crisis. Traditional financial systems had failed, and people were seeking alternatives. Enter Satoshi Nakamoto, an enigmatic figure whose true identity remains unknown. In 2009, Nakamoto released the first blockchain-based cryptocurrency, Bitcoin. This marked the beginning of a technological revolution.

At its core, blockchain is a decentralized ledger of all transactions across a network. This ledger is not stored in a single location but distributed across many computers, making it incredibly secure and transparent. Each transaction is recorded in a "block," and these blocks are linked together in a "chain"—hence the name, blockchain.

Understanding the Basics

To understand blockchain, we need to grasp a few fundamental concepts:

- **Decentralization**: Unlike traditional databases managed by a central authority, a blockchain is maintained by a network of nodes (computers). Each node has a copy of the entire blockchain, ensuring that no single point of failure exists.
- **Transparency**: Every transaction on a blockchain is visible to all participants. This transparency builds trust, as anyone can verify the data independently.
- **Immutability**: Once a block is added to the chain, it cannot be altered. This feature ensures the integrity and security of the data.
- **Consensus Mechanisms**: For transactions to be added to the blockchain, the network must agree on their validity. This is achieved through various consensus mechanisms, such as Proof of Work (PoW) and Proof of Stake (PoS).

The Mechanics of Blockchain

Let's delve deeper into how a blockchain functions. Imagine Alice wants to send some cryptocurrency to Bob. Here's what happens:

- **Transaction Creation**: Alice initiates a transaction, which includes details such as the amount and the recipient's address.
- **Broadcasting**: This transaction is broadcast to the entire network of nodes.
- **Validation**: The nodes validate the transaction using the chosen consensus mechanism. For example, in Bitcoin's PoW system, miners compete to solve a complex mathematical puzzle. The first one to solve it gets to add the block to the blockchain and is rewarded with cryptocurrency.

- **Block Addition**: Once validated, the transaction is added to a block. This block is then appended to the existing blockchain.
- **Confirmation**: Bob receives the cryptocurrency, and the transaction is confirmed across the network.

Real-World Applications

While cryptocurrencies like Bitcoin and Ethereum are the most well-known applications of blockchain, the technology's potential extends far beyond digital currencies. Here are a few areas where blockchain is making waves:

- **Supply Chain Management**: Blockchain can enhance transparency and traceability in supply chains. Companies can track the journey of products from origin to consumer, ensuring authenticity and reducing fraud.
- **Healthcare**: Patient records can be securely stored and shared on a blockchain, improving access to medical history and ensuring privacy.
- **Voting Systems**: Blockchain can create tamper-proof voting systems, ensuring fair and transparent elections.
- **Real Estate**: Property transactions can be streamlined with blockchain, reducing paperwork and preventing fraud.
- **Smart Contracts**: These self-executing contracts with the terms directly written into code can automate and enforce agreements without intermediaries.

The Road Ahead

Blockchain technology is still in its infancy, but its potential is immense. As we continue to explore and innovate, new applications and improvements will emerge. However, the journey is not without challenges. Scalability, energy consumption, and regulatory hurdles are significant obstacles that need addressing.

In the coming chapters, we will dive deeper into these aspects, exploring the intricacies of blockchain technology, its various use cases, and the future it promises. We will meet pioneers in the field, unravel complex concepts, and understand how this technology can transform our world.

So, fasten your seatbelt and get ready to embark on a journey through the fascinating world of blockchain. This is just the beginning. The future is decentralized, and it starts here.

1.1. What is Blockchain?

To truly grasp the revolutionary potential of blockchain technology, it's essential to start with a clear understanding of what blockchain is and how it operates. At its most basic level, blockchain is a type of distributed ledger technology (DLT). This means it is a digital system for recording transactions and related data in multiple places at once. Unlike traditional ledgers, which are typically centralized and controlled by a single entity, a blockchain ledger is decentralized and maintained by a network of computers, known as nodes.

The Structure of a Blockchain

A blockchain is composed of a series of blocks, each containing a list of transactions. These blocks are linked together chronologically in a chain, creating a secure and immutable record of all transactions that have occurred on the network. Here's how this structure works in more detail:

1. **Blocks**: Each block in the blockchain contains three main elements:

   - **Data**: This is the transaction information, which can vary depending on the blockchain's purpose. For instance, in the Bitcoin blockchain, this data includes sender and receiver details and the amount of cryptocurrency transferred.
   - **Hash**: A hash is a unique identifier for each block. It's created using a cryptographic function that takes the block's data and generates a fixed-length string of characters. This ensures the block's contents cannot be altered without changing the hash.
   - **Previous Block's Hash**: Each block contains the hash of the previous block in the chain, linking them together. This interconnectedness ensures the security and integrity of the entire blockchain, as altering any block would require changing every subsequent block.

2. **Decentralization**: Unlike traditional databases, which are stored on a single server or a group of servers controlled by a central entity, a blockchain is distributed across a network of nodes. Each node maintains a complete copy of the blockchain and participates in the validation and verification of new transactions. This

decentralized nature removes the need for intermediaries and central authorities, enhancing security and reducing the risk of fraud.

3. **Consensus Mechanisms**: For a new block to be added to the blockchain, the network must reach a consensus on its validity. This is achieved through various consensus mechanisms, which are protocols that ensure all nodes agree on the state of the blockchain. Two of the most common consensus mechanisms are:

- **Proof of Work (PoW)**: Used by Bitcoin, PoW requires nodes (miners) to solve complex mathematical puzzles to validate transactions and add new blocks. This process is resource-intensive but provides strong security.
- **Proof of Stake (PoS)**: PoS selects validators based on the number of coins they hold and are willing to "stake" as collateral. This method is more energy-efficient than PoW and is used by several newer blockchains.

The Key Characteristics of Blockchain

Blockchain technology has several defining characteristics that distinguish it from other types of databases and ledger systems:

- **Immutability**: Once a block is added to the blockchain, it is nearly impossible to alter. Any attempt to change a block would require altering all subsequent blocks, which would be immediately detected by the network. This immutability ensures the integrity and trustworthiness of the data recorded on the blockchain.

- **Transparency**: All transactions recorded on a public blockchain are visible to anyone with access to the network. This transparency allows for easy verification of transactions and fosters trust among participants. However, there are also private blockchains where access and visibility are restricted to certain participants.
- **Security**: Blockchain's decentralized and cryptographic nature provides robust security. Each block is linked to the previous block using cryptographic hashes, creating a chain that is highly resistant to tampering. Additionally, the decentralized network of nodes ensures that no single point of failure exists, making it difficult for malicious actors to compromise the system.

Practical Example: How a Blockchain Transaction Works

To illustrate how blockchain works, let's follow a simple transaction on the Bitcoin blockchain:

- **Initiation**: Alice wants to send 1 Bitcoin to Bob. She initiates the transaction using her digital wallet, which creates a transaction message containing Bob's public address and the amount of Bitcoin to be sent.
- **Broadcasting**: The transaction message is broadcasted to the entire Bitcoin network, where it is received by nodes.
- **Validation**: Nodes validate the transaction by checking that Alice has sufficient Bitcoin to send and that the transaction message is correctly formatted. In the Bitcoin network, miners then compete to solve a cryptographic puzzle as part of the PoW consensus mechanism.

- **Block Creation**: The first miner to solve the puzzle adds the validated transaction to a new block, which is then added to the blockchain. This new block includes the hash of the previous block, creating a continuous chain.
- **Confirmation**: Once the block is added to the blockchain, the transaction is considered confirmed. Bob can now see that he has received 1 Bitcoin from Alice.

Blockchain technology represents a paradigm shift in how we think about data, transactions, and trust. By decentralizing control and leveraging cryptographic principles, blockchain offers a secure, transparent, and immutable way to record and verify transactions. As we explore further in this book, you'll see how these fundamental principles are applied across various industries, unlocking new possibilities and transforming the way we interact with the digital world.

1.2. The History and Evolution of Blockchain

Blockchain technology, though a relatively recent innovation, has roots that trace back several decades. Its development has been marked by groundbreaking ideas, influential projects, and gradual evolution, leading to the robust and versatile technology we recognize today. This chapter delves into the fascinating history and evolution of blockchain, from its conceptual origins to its current applications and future potential.

Early Conceptual Origins

The foundational ideas behind blockchain can be traced back to the late 20th century, primarily in the fields of cryptography and computer science.

- **Merkle Trees (1979)**: One of the earliest contributions to blockchain technology came from Ralph Merkle, who introduced the concept of Merkle Trees. These data structures allow efficient and secure verification of the contents of large data sets. Merkle Trees are a critical component of blockchain technology, enabling the efficient and secure handling of transactions.
- **Cryptographic Hash Functions (1970s-1980s)**: Throughout the 1970s and 1980s, cryptographic hash functions were developed and refined. These functions take an input (or 'message') and return a fixed-size string of bytes, which appears random. Hash functions are essential for ensuring the integrity and security of data in a blockchain.
- **Digital Cash (1980s-1990s)**: In the late 1980s and early 1990s, cryptographer David Chaum introduced the concept of digital cash with his company DigiCash. Although DigiCash ultimately did not succeed commercially, it laid the groundwork for later developments in digital currency and blockchain technology.

The Birth of Bitcoin and Blockchain

The true birth of blockchain technology came in 2008, with the release of a white paper titled "Bitcoin: A Peer-to-Peer Electronic Cash System" by the pseudonymous Satoshi Nakamoto.

- **Bitcoin White Paper (2008)**: Satoshi Nakamoto's white paper proposed a decentralized digital currency that would allow secure, peer-to-peer transactions without the need for a trusted third party. This paper introduced the key concepts of blockchain technology, including the use of a decentralized ledger, proof of work, and cryptographic security.
- **Genesis Block (2009)**: On January 3, 2009, Nakamoto mined the first block of the Bitcoin blockchain, known as the Genesis Block. This marked the official launch of the Bitcoin network and the first practical implementation of blockchain technology.
- **Early Adoption and Growth (2009-2013)**: In its early years, Bitcoin was primarily adopted by a niche community of cryptographers, technologists, and libertarians. The first real-world Bitcoin transaction took place in 2010 when a programmer named Laszlo Hanyecz famously paid 10,000 bitcoins for two pizzas. As Bitcoin began to gain attention, its value and user base grew, leading to increased interest and investment in blockchain technology.

The Rise of Altcoins and Blockchain 2.0

As Bitcoin gained popularity, developers and entrepreneurs recognized the potential for blockchain technology to support a wide range of applications beyond digital currency.

- **Altcoins (2011-Present)**: The first alternative cryptocurrencies, or "altcoins," began to emerge in 2011. These included Litecoin, Namecoin, and many others. Altcoins sought to improve Bitcoin's design by offering features such as faster transaction times, enhanced privacy, and new consensus mechanisms.

- **Ethereum and Smart Contracts (2015)**: Perhaps the most significant development in the evolution of blockchain technology was the launch of Ethereum in 2015. Created by Vitalik Buterin, Ethereum introduced the concept of smart contracts—self-executing contracts with the terms of the agreement directly written into code. Ethereum's blockchain-enabled developers build decentralized applications (DApps) on top of its platform, vastly expanding the potential use cases for blockchain technology.

Blockchain 3.0 and Beyond

The ongoing evolution of blockchain technology is characterized by efforts to address its limitations and expand its capabilities.

- **Scalability Solutions**: One of the primary challenges facing blockchain technology is scalability. As more users and transactions are added to a blockchain, the network can become slow and congested. Various solutions have been proposed and implemented to address this issue, including:
- **Sharding**: Dividing the blockchain into smaller, more manageable pieces (shards) that can be processed in parallel.
- **Layer 2 Solutions**: Implementing off-chain solutions, such as the Lightning Network for Bitcoin, which allow transactions to be processed outside of the main blockchain.
- **Interoperability**: As multiple blockchains have emerged, the need for interoperability between them has become increasingly important. Projects like Polkadot and Cosmos aim to create frameworks that enable different blockchains to communicate and interact with each other seamlessly.

- **Decentralized Finance (DeFi)**: DeFi represents one of the most exciting and rapidly growing areas of blockchain application. DeFi platforms leverage smart contracts to create decentralized financial services, including lending, borrowing, trading, and earning interest, without the need for traditional financial intermediaries.
- **Non-Fungible Tokens (NFTs)**: NFTs have gained significant attention as a way to represent ownership of unique digital assets on the blockchain. NFTs have been used for a variety of purposes, including digital art, collectibles, gaming assets, and more.

The Future of Blockchain

As blockchain technology continues to evolve, its potential applications are virtually limitless. Industries such as healthcare, supply chain management, real estate, and governance are exploring ways to leverage blockchain to improve transparency, efficiency, and security. Additionally, ongoing research and development aim to address current limitations and unlock new possibilities for innovation.

1.3. Key Concepts and Terminologies

To navigate the world of blockchain effectively, it's crucial to understand the key concepts and terminologies that form the foundation of this revolutionary technology. In this chapter, we'll explore the essential terms and ideas that you'll encounter as you delve deeper into blockchain.

1. Cryptography

Cryptography forms the backbone of blockchain technology, providing the tools and techniques necessary to secure transactions and data on the network.

- **Public Key Cryptography**: Also known as asymmetric cryptography, this method uses a pair of keys—a public key and a private key—to encrypt and decrypt data. Public keys are shared openly, allowing anyone to encrypt messages intended for the owner of the corresponding private key.
- **Hash Functions**: Cryptographic hash functions take an input (or 'message') and produce a fixed-size string of characters, known as a hash. Hash functions have several important properties, including determinism (the same input always produces the same output) and collision resistance (it's computationally infeasible to find two different inputs that produce the same hash).

2. Decentralization

Decentralization is a core principle of blockchain technology, representing a departure from traditional centralized systems controlled by a single authority.

- **Nodes**: Nodes are individual computers or devices that participate in the blockchain network. Each node stores a copy of the entire blockchain and contributes to the validation and propagation of transactions.

- **Consensus Mechanisms**: Consensus mechanisms are protocols that enable nodes to agree on the state of the blockchain. Popular consensus mechanisms include Proof of Work (PoW), Proof of Stake (PoS), and Delegated Proof of Stake (DPoS).

3. Immutable Ledger

The immutable ledger maintained by blockchain ensures the integrity and transparency of transactions recorded on the network.

- **Blocks**: Blocks are containers that hold a collection of transactions. Each block is cryptographically linked to the previous block, forming a chain that cannot be altered without invalidating subsequent blocks.
- **Timestamps**: Each block in the blockchain contains a timestamp, indicating when the block was created. This timestamp helps establish the chronological order of transactions.

4. Smart Contracts

Smart contracts are self-executing contracts with the terms of the agreement directly written into code.

- **Ethereum Virtual Machine (EVM)**: The Ethereum Virtual Machine is a decentralized runtime environment that executes smart contracts on the Ethereum blockchain.

- **Gas**: Gas is the unit of computation used to execute operations and run smart contracts on the Ethereum network. Users must pay gas fees to compensate miners for processing their transactions.

5. Tokenization

Tokenization involves representing real-world assets or digital rights as digital tokens on a blockchain.

- **Utility Tokens**: Utility tokens provide access to a specific product or service within a blockchain ecosystem.
- **Security Tokens**: Security tokens represent ownership of a tradable asset, such as equity in a company or real estate. Security tokens are subject to securities regulations.

These key concepts and terminologies provide a solid foundation for understanding blockchain technology and its applications. As we delve deeper into specific topics and use cases in subsequent chapters, you'll encounter these terms frequently. By mastering these fundamentals, you'll be better equipped to explore the exciting and rapidly evolving world of blockchain.

1.4. How Blockchain Works: An Overview

Understanding how blockchain works is essential for grasping its transformative potential. In this chapter, we'll provide an overview of the underlying mechanisms that power blockchain technology and enable its decentralized, secure, and transparent operation.

1. Data Structure: Blocks and Chains

At its core, a blockchain is a distributed ledger that records transactions in a series of blocks. Each block contains a batch of transactions and is linked to the previous block, forming a chain. This structure ensures that transactions are recorded in chronological order and cannot be altered retroactively.

- **Blocks**: Each block in the blockchain contains data about transactions, such as the sender, receiver, and amount transferred. Additionally, each block includes a unique identifier called a hash, which is generated based on the block's contents.
- **Chains**: The blocks in a blockchain are linked together using cryptographic hashes. Each block contains the hash of the previous block, creating a continuous chain. This linkage ensures the integrity and immutability of the blockchain.

2. Decentralization and Consensus

Blockchain operates on a decentralized network of nodes, each of which maintains a copy of the blockchain and participates in the validation of transactions. Consensus mechanisms ensure that all nodes agree on the state of the blockchain and the validity of new transactions.

- **Nodes**: Nodes are individual computers or devices that participate in the blockchain network. Nodes store a copy of the entire blockchain and communicate with other nodes to propagate transactions and blocks.
- **Consensus Mechanisms**: Consensus mechanisms are protocols that enable nodes to agree on the state of the blockchain. Popular consensus mechanisms include Proof of Work (PoW), Proof of Stake (PoS), and Delegated Proof of Stake (DPoS). These mechanisms ensure that the majority of nodes reach a consensus on which transactions are valid and should be added to the blockchain.

3. Security and Immutability

Blockchain technology provides robust security and immutability, ensuring that transactions are tamper-proof and resistant to unauthorized changes.

- **Cryptographic Hashing**: Cryptographic hash functions are used to generate unique identifiers (hashes) for each block. These hashes are cryptographically linked, making it computationally infeasible to alter the contents of a block without changing its hash.
- **Immutable Ledger**: Once a block is added to the blockchain, it becomes part of a permanent, immutable record. Altering a single block would require changing the hashes of all subsequent blocks, which is practically impossible due to the computational resources required.

4. Transaction Lifecycle

Transactions in a blockchain network follow a predefined lifecycle, from initiation to confirmation and recording on the blockchain.

- **Initiation**: A user initiates a transaction by creating a transaction message containing details such as the sender, receiver, and amount.
- **Validation**: Nodes in the network validate the transaction to ensure that it meets the criteria defined by the consensus mechanism. Valid transactions are added to a new block.
- **Confirmation**: Once added to a block, the transaction is considered confirmed. Subsequent blocks are added to the blockchain, further securing the transaction and making it increasingly difficult to reverse.

Blockchain technology revolutionizes how transactions are recorded, verified, and secured in a decentralized and transparent manner. By understanding the fundamental principles of blockchain operation, you'll be better equipped to explore its diverse applications across various industries and unlock its full potential for innovation and disruption.

1.5. The Importance of Blockchain in Today's World

In today's rapidly evolving digital landscape, blockchain technology has emerged as a groundbreaking innovation with far-reaching implications across diverse industries. Its decentralized, transparent, and secure nature has positioned blockchain as a catalyst for transformative change, offering solutions to some of the most pressing challenges facing our world. In this chapter, we'll explore the significance of blockchain in today's world and its potential to reshape economies, societies, and the way we interact with technology.

1. Decentralization and Trust

At the heart of blockchain's importance lies its ability to decentralize control and establish trust in environments where trust is traditionally lacking.

- **Financial Inclusion**: In regions with limited access to traditional banking services, blockchain-powered financial systems can provide a pathway to financial inclusion. By bypassing intermediaries and enabling peer-to-peer transactions, blockchain opens up new opportunities for individuals and businesses to participate in the global economy.
- **Transparency and Accountability**: Blockchain's transparent and immutable ledger ensures that transactions are recorded and verified in a tamper-proof manner. This transparency fosters accountability and reduces the risk of fraud, corruption, and manipulation in various sectors, including finance, supply chain management, and governance.

2. Security and Data Integrity

Blockchain technology offers robust security and data integrity, mitigating the risks associated with centralized systems and enhancing privacy protection.

- **Cybersecurity**: The decentralized nature of blockchain networks makes them resistant to cyberattacks and single points of failure. By distributing data across a network of nodes and encrypting transactions using cryptographic techniques, blockchain reduces the vulnerability of sensitive information to hacking and unauthorized access.
- **Data Ownership and Privacy**: With blockchain, individuals have greater control over their data and digital identities. Through self-sovereign identity solutions and decentralized authentication mechanisms, blockchain empowers users to manage their personal information securely and selectively share it with trusted parties, enhancing privacy protection and reducing the risk of data breaches.

3. Innovation and Disruption

Blockchain technology fuels innovation and disruption across industries, unlocking new possibilities for efficiency, transparency, and collaboration.

- **Supply Chain Management**: Blockchain enables end-to-end traceability and transparency in supply chains, allowing stakeholders to track the journey of products from origin to consumer. By recording immutable data about each stage of the supply chain, blockchain reduces the risk of counterfeit goods, improves product quality, and enhances trust between partners.
- **Decentralized Finance (DeFi)**: DeFi platforms built on blockchain enable decentralized access to financial services such as lending, borrowing, and trading. By removing intermediaries and automating transactions through smart contracts, DeFi

promotes financial inclusion, reduces transaction costs, and increases the efficiency of capital allocation.

4. Social Impact and Empowerment

Beyond its technological advancements, blockchain has the potential to drive positive social impact and empower marginalized communities worldwide.

- **Remittances and Cross-Border Payments**: Blockchain-powered remittance platforms offer a cost-effective and efficient alternative to traditional money transfer services, particularly for migrant workers sending money to their families in developing countries. By reducing transaction fees and processing times, blockchain facilitates financial support and economic empowerment for underserved populations.
- **Identity Management**: Blockchain-based identity solutions provide secure and portable digital identities for individuals lacking official documentation or facing identity-related challenges. By enabling access to essential services such as healthcare, education, and financial services, blockchain empowers individuals to assert their rights and participate fully in society.

The importance of blockchain in today's world cannot be overstated. As we confront complex global challenges ranging from economic inequality and data breaches to environmental degradation and social injustice, blockchain offers a ray of hope—a decentralized, transparent, and secure foundation upon which we can build a more equitable, sustainable, and inclusive future. By harnessing the power of blockchain technology, we can unlock new opportunities for innovation, collaboration, and positive social change, shaping a world where trust, transparency, and empowerment are the cornerstones of progress.

Chapter 2: Understanding Bitcoin and Cryptocurrency

In this chapter, we'll delve into the fascinating world of Bitcoin and cryptocurrency, exploring their origins, underlying technology, and impact on the global financial landscape. From its humble beginnings to its status as a revolutionary digital asset, Bitcoin has captured the imagination of millions worldwide and paved the way for the emergence of a new era of decentralized finance. Let's embark on a journey to understand the fundamentals of Bitcoin and cryptocurrency.

1. The Birth of Bitcoin

Bitcoin, the world's first decentralized cryptocurrency, was introduced to the world in 2008 by an enigmatic figure known as Satoshi Nakamoto. Nakamoto's white paper, titled "Bitcoin: A Peer-to-Peer Electronic Cash System," outlined a vision for a digital currency that would enable secure, peer-to-peer transactions without the need for intermediaries or centralized control.

- **Genesis Block**: On January 3, 2009, Nakamoto mined the first block of the Bitcoin blockchain, known as the Genesis Block. This marked the official launch of the Bitcoin network and the beginning of a revolutionary experiment in decentralized finance.
- **Proof of Work**: Bitcoin operates on a consensus mechanism known as Proof of Work (PoW), where miners compete to solve complex mathematical puzzles to validate transactions and add new blocks to the blockchain. This process ensures the security and integrity of the Bitcoin network.

2. How Bitcoin Works

Bitcoin operates on a decentralized network of nodes, each maintaining a copy of the blockchain and participating in the validation of transactions. Transactions are recorded on the blockchain in blocks, which are linked together chronologically, forming a continuous chain.

- **Digital Signatures**: Bitcoin transactions are secured using digital signatures, which provide cryptographic proof of ownership and authorization. Each user has a public key and a private key, which they use to sign transactions and prove ownership of their Bitcoin holdings.
- **Mining and Block Rewards**: Miners play a crucial role in the Bitcoin network, validating transactions and adding new blocks to the blockchain. In return for their efforts, miners are rewarded with newly minted bitcoins and transaction fees.

3. The Rise of Cryptocurrency

Bitcoin's success paved the way for the emergence of thousands of alternative cryptocurrencies, collectively known as altcoins. These digital assets seek to improve Bitcoin's design by offering features such as faster transaction times, enhanced privacy, and new consensus mechanisms.

- **Altcoins**: Litecoin, Ethereum, Ripple, and many others are examples of popular altcoins that have gained traction in the cryptocurrency market. Each altcoin has its unique features and use cases, catering to different needs and preferences within the crypto community.

- **Smart Contracts**: Ethereum, in particular, introduced the concept of smart contracts—self-executing contracts with the terms of the agreement directly written into code. Smart contracts enable a wide range of decentralized applications (DApps) and have fueled the growth of decentralized finance (DeFi).

4. The Impact of Cryptocurrency

Cryptocurrency has had a profound impact on the global financial landscape, challenging traditional banking systems and reshaping the way we think about money and value transfer.

- **Financial Inclusion**: Cryptocurrency has the potential to provide financial services to underserved populations worldwide, enabling peer-to-peer transactions and bypassing traditional banking infrastructure.
- **Decentralized Finance (DeFi)**: DeFi platforms built on blockchain enable decentralized access to financial services such as lending, borrowing, and trading. By removing intermediaries and automating transactions through smart contracts, DeFi promotes financial inclusion and empowers individuals to control their financial assets.

Bitcoin and cryptocurrency represent a paradigm shift in how we think about money, finance, and value exchange. From its humble beginnings as an experimental digital currency to its status as a global phenomenon, Bitcoin has paved the way for a new era of decentralized finance and innovation. As we continue to explore the potential of cryptocurrency and blockchain technology, we must navigate the opportunities and challenges they present, striving to build a more inclusive, transparent, and equitable financial system for all.

2.1. What is Bitcoin?

Bitcoin is the world's first decentralized cryptocurrency, introduced to the world in 2008 by an anonymous entity known as Satoshi Nakamoto. At its core, Bitcoin is a digital currency that operates on a peer-to-peer network, allowing users to send and receive payments without the need for intermediaries such as banks or payment processors.

Key Characteristics of Bitcoin:

- **Decentralization**: Bitcoin operates on a decentralized network of computers, known as nodes, which collectively maintain the integrity of the blockchain—the public ledger that records all Bitcoin transactions. This decentralized nature means that no single entity has control over the Bitcoin network, making it resistant to censorship and manipulation.
- **Limited Supply**: Unlike traditional fiat currencies, which can be printed at will by central banks, Bitcoin has a finite supply. The total number of bitcoins that will ever exist is capped at 21 million, ensuring scarcity and protecting against inflation.
- **Security**: Bitcoin transactions are secured using cryptographic techniques, making them resistant to fraud and counterfeiting. Each transaction is verified by multiple nodes on the network

before being added to the blockchain, providing a high level of security and trust.

- **Pseudonymity**: While Bitcoin transactions are recorded on a public ledger, the identities of the parties involved are not directly tied to their Bitcoin addresses. Instead, users are represented by alphanumeric strings, providing a degree of privacy and pseudonymity.
- **Irreversibility**: Once a Bitcoin transaction is confirmed and added to the blockchain, it is irreversible. This means that once a payment is sent, it cannot be undone or reversed, providing finality and security for both buyers and sellers.

How Bitcoin Works:

Bitcoin transactions are initiated by users who create digital messages containing details such as the sender, receiver, and amount of Bitcoin to be transferred. These transactions are broadcast to the Bitcoin network, where they are validated by nodes using a consensus mechanism known as Proof of Work (PoW).

Miners, who are specialized nodes on the network, compete to solve complex mathematical puzzles to validate transactions and add new blocks to the blockchain. In return for their efforts, miners are rewarded with newly minted bitcoins and transaction fees.

Once a transaction is validated and added to a block, it becomes part of the immutable blockchain, where it can be viewed by anyone with access to the network. This transparent and decentralized ledger ensures the integrity and security of the Bitcoin network.

In summary, Bitcoin is a revolutionary digital currency that offers decentralized, secure, and transparent peer-to-peer transactions. As the first and most well-known cryptocurrency, Bitcoin has paved the way for the emergence of a new era of digital finance and innovation.

2.2. The Rise of Bitcoin: A Brief History

The journey of Bitcoin from its humble beginnings to its status as a global phenomenon is a tale of innovation, experimentation, and resilience. In this section, we'll explore the key milestones and events that have shaped the remarkable rise of Bitcoin.

1. **Genesis of Bitcoin (2008-2009)**

- **White Paper**: In October 2008, a mysterious individual or group known as Satoshi Nakamoto published a white paper titled "Bitcoin: A Peer-to-Peer Electronic Cash System." This seminal document outlined the principles of a decentralized digital currency that would enable secure, peer-to-peer transactions without the need for intermediaries.
- **Genesis Block**: On January 3, 2009, Nakamoto mined the first block of the Bitcoin blockchain, known as the Genesis Block. This marked the official launch of the Bitcoin network and the beginning of a revolutionary experiment in decentralized finance.

2. **Early Adopters and Enthusiasts (2009-2013)**

- **Mining and Distribution**: In the early days of Bitcoin, mining was accessible to anyone with a computer and an internet connection. Early adopters mined large quantities of bitcoins at relatively low difficulty levels, accumulating significant wealth in the process.

- **First Transactions**: The first real-world Bitcoin transaction took place on May 22, 2010, when programmer Laszlo Hanyecz famously paid 10,000 Bitcoins for two pizzas. This event commemorated as Bitcoin Pizza Day, marked a significant milestone in Bitcoin's journey as a medium of exchange.

3. Mainstream Recognition and Volatility (2013-2017)

- **Media Attention**: Bitcoin began to attract mainstream attention in 2013, as its price surged to over $1,000 for the first time. Media coverage and investor interest fueled a speculative frenzy, leading to rapid price fluctuations and increased volatility.
- **Regulatory Challenges**: As Bitcoin gained prominence, it also faced regulatory scrutiny from governments and financial authorities worldwide. Concerns about money laundering, tax evasion, and the use of Bitcoin for illicit activities led to regulatory crackdowns and restrictions in some jurisdictions.

4. Institutional Adoption and Maturation (2017-Present)

- **Institutional Investment**: In recent years, Bitcoin has gained legitimacy as an investable asset class, attracting institutional investors and hedge funds seeking exposure to digital assets. High-profile endorsements from companies like Tesla and Square have further bolstered Bitcoin's credibility.

- **Market Maturity**: The Bitcoin market has matured significantly, with the emergence of regulated exchanges, derivatives markets, and investment products such as Bitcoin exchange-traded funds (ETFs). These developments have increased liquidity and accessibility for investors seeking exposure to Bitcoin.

5. Continued Innovation and Adoption (Present and Beyond)

- **Technological Advancements**: Ongoing research and development efforts are focused on improving the scalability, privacy, and functionality of the Bitcoin network. Initiatives such as the Lightning Network aim to enable faster and more cost-effective transactions, enhancing Bitcoin's utility as a medium of exchange.
- **Global Adoption**: Bitcoin adoption continues to grow worldwide, with increasing acceptance by merchants, businesses, and individuals as a form of payment. In countries facing economic instability or hyperinflation, Bitcoin offers a store of value and a hedge against currency depreciation.

The rise of Bitcoin from obscurity to prominence is a testament to the power of decentralized technology and the resilience of the human spirit. Despite facing skepticism, criticism, and regulatory challenges, Bitcoin has emerged as a transformative force in global finance, offering an alternative to traditional banking systems and fiat currencies. As Bitcoin's journey continues, its impact on the world of finance and technology is likely to be felt for generations to come.

2.3. How Bitcoin Works: Blockchain and Mining

Bitcoin operates on a decentralized network powered by blockchain technology—a distributed ledger that records all transactions securely and transparently. In this section, we'll explore the core components of Bitcoin's infrastructure, including the blockchain and the mining process.

1. Blockchain: The Backbone of Bitcoin

- **Definition**: The blockchain is a decentralized ledger that maintains a record of all Bitcoin transactions. Each transaction is grouped into blocks, which are cryptographically linked together to form a continuous chain.
- **Data Structure**: A block contains a batch of transactions, along with metadata such as timestamps and transaction fees. Each block also includes a unique identifier called a hash, which is generated based on the block's contents.
- **Decentralization and Security**: The blockchain is maintained by a network of nodes, each of which stores a copy of the entire blockchain. This decentralized architecture ensures that no single entity has control over the Bitcoin network, making it resistant to censorship and tampering.

2. Mining: Securing the Network

- **Proof of Work (PoW)**: Bitcoin mining is the process by which new bitcoins are created and transactions are validated and added to the blockchain. Miners compete to solve complex mathematical puzzles, known as hash functions, using computational power.

- **Block Validation**: Miners collect transactions from the Bitcoin mempool and package them into blocks. They then attempt to find a nonce—a random number—that, when combined with the block's contents, produces a hash with a specific number of leading zeros.
- **Mining Rewards**: The first miner to successfully find a valid nonce and solve the puzzle receives a reward in the form of newly minted bitcoins, as well as transaction fees from the included transactions. This process incentivizes miners to contribute computational power to secure the network.

3. Blockchain Consensus: Achieving Agreement

- **Consensus Mechanism**: Bitcoin's blockchain achieves consensus among nodes through the Proof of Work (PoW) consensus mechanism. Nodes validate transactions and blocks based on cryptographic principles, ensuring agreement on the state of the blockchain.
- **Longest Chain Rule**: In the event of conflicting blocks, nodes on the Bitcoin network adhere to the longest chain rule, accepting the chain with the most cumulative proof of work as the valid blockchain. This mechanism helps prevent double-spending and ensures the integrity of the network.

Bitcoin's operation relies on the synergy between its blockchain and mining processes. The blockchain serves as a decentralized ledger, recording all transactions securely and transparently. Mining, powered by the Proof of Work consensus mechanism, ensures the security and integrity of the network by validating transactions and adding new blocks to the blockchain. Together, these components form the backbone of the Bitcoin network, enabling peer-to-peer transactions and maintaining the trust and decentralization that define Bitcoin's revolutionary ethos.

2.4. Other Popular Cryptocurrencies: Ethereum, Litecoin, and More

While Bitcoin was the first cryptocurrency to gain widespread recognition, it has since been joined by a multitude of alternative cryptocurrencies, often referred to as "altcoins." In this section, we'll explore some of the most notable altcoins, including Ethereum, Litecoin, and others, and examine their unique features and contributions to the cryptocurrency ecosystem.

1. Ethereum (ETH)

- **Smart Contracts**: Ethereum, launched in 2015 by Vitalik Buterin, introduced the concept of smart contracts—self-executing contracts with the terms of the agreement directly written into code. Smart contracts enable developers to build decentralized applications (DApps) on the Ethereum blockchain, revolutionizing the way we interact with digital assets and conduct transactions.
- **Decentralized Finance (DeFi)**: Ethereum has become the foundation for the burgeoning decentralized finance (DeFi) movement, which seeks to recreate traditional financial services such as lending, borrowing, and trading on blockchain networks. DeFi platforms built on Ethereum enable peer-to-peer financial

transactions without intermediaries, offering increased transparency, efficiency, and accessibility.

2. Litecoin (LTC)

- **Faster Transactions**: Created by Charlie Lee in 2011, Litecoin is often referred to as the "silver to Bitcoin's gold." Litecoin was designed to be a faster and more lightweight alternative to Bitcoin, with a shorter block generation time and a larger maximum supply. These features make Litecoin well-suited for everyday transactions and micropayments.
- **Scrypt Algorithm**: Unlike Bitcoin, which uses the SHA-256 hashing algorithm for mining, Litecoin employs the Scrypt algorithm. This algorithm is memory-intensive rather than CPU-intensive, making it more resistant to specialized mining hardware known as ASICs and promoting decentralization.

3. Ripple (XRP)

- **Cross-Border Payments**: Ripple, created in 2012 by Ripple Labs, aims to facilitate fast and low-cost cross-border payments for financial institutions. The Ripple network operates on a consensus protocol known as the Ripple Protocol Consensus Algorithm (RPCA), which enables near-instant settlement of transactions with minimal fees.
- **Centralized Governance**: Ripple's approach to decentralization differs from that of Bitcoin and Ethereum. While Bitcoin and Ethereum rely on decentralized networks of nodes to validate transactions, Ripple employs a more centralized governance

model, with Ripple Labs exerting significant influence over the network.

4. Cardano (ADA)

- **Proof of Stake (PoS)**: Cardano, founded by Charles Hoskinson, is a blockchain platform known for its scientific approach to development and emphasis on sustainability and scalability. Cardano utilizes a Proof of Stake (PoS) consensus mechanism, which requires participants to hold a stake in the network to validate transactions and create new blocks.
- **Scalability and Interoperability**: Cardano aims to address the scalability and interoperability challenges faced by existing blockchain platforms. Through its modular architecture and ongoing research efforts, Cardano seeks to achieve high throughput and seamless interoperability with other blockchain networks.

These are just a few examples of the diverse range of cryptocurrencies that have emerged since the inception of Bitcoin. Each cryptocurrency brings its unique features, use cases, and vision for the future of decentralized finance and technology. As the cryptocurrency ecosystem continues to evolve, we can expect to see further innovation, experimentation, and disruption, shaping the future of finance and technology in profound ways.

2.5. The Role of Cryptocurrency in the Modern Financial System

Cryptocurrency has emerged as a disruptive force in the modern financial system, challenging traditional banking models and reshaping the way we think about money, value transfer, and financial transactions. In this section, we'll explore the evolving role of cryptocurrency in the modern financial landscape and its potential to revolutionize the way we conduct financial transactions, invest, and store value.

1. Financial Inclusion and Accessibility

- **Global Reach**: Cryptocurrency has the potential to provide financial services to underserved populations worldwide, including the unbanked and underbanked. By leveraging blockchain technology, individuals in remote or economically disadvantaged areas can access banking services and participate in the global economy without relying on traditional financial institutions.
- **Low-Cost Transactions**: Cryptocurrency transactions often incur lower fees compared to traditional banking systems, particularly for cross-border payments. This makes cryptocurrency an attractive option for individuals and businesses seeking to reduce transaction costs and streamline international money transfers.

2. Decentralization and Trust

- **Decentralized Finance (DeFi)**: Cryptocurrency has fueled the growth of decentralized finance (DeFi) platforms, which aim to recreate traditional financial services such as lending, borrowing, and trading on blockchain networks. DeFi platforms operate without intermediaries, providing increased transparency, efficiency, and accessibility for users.

- **Trustless Transactions**: Blockchain technology enables trustless transactions, meaning that parties can transact with each other without the need for a trusted intermediary. Smart contracts, self-executing contracts with the terms of the agreement directly written into code, automate transactions and enforce agreements without relying on third parties.

3. **Store of Value and Investment**

- **Hedge against Inflation**: Cryptocurrency, particularly Bitcoin, has emerged as a store of value and a hedge against inflation in times of economic uncertainty. The finite supply of cryptocurrencies, coupled with their decentralized nature, makes them resistant to government manipulation and currency depreciation.
- **Investment Opportunities**: Cryptocurrency has created new investment opportunities for individuals seeking exposure to digital assets. Institutional investors, hedge funds, and retail investors alike are increasingly allocating capital to cryptocurrencies as part of their investment portfolios, viewing them as a diversification strategy and a potential source of high returns.

4. Regulatory Challenges and Uncertainty

- **Regulatory Scrutiny**: Cryptocurrency faces regulatory scrutiny from governments and financial authorities worldwide, due to concerns about money laundering, tax evasion, and the use of cryptocurrency for illicit activities. Regulatory uncertainty and inconsistent treatment of cryptocurrencies by different jurisdictions pose challenges for adoption and mainstream integration.
- **Market Volatility**: Cryptocurrency markets are known for their volatility, with prices subject to rapid fluctuations driven by factors such as market sentiment, regulatory developments, and technological innovations. While volatility can present opportunities for traders and investors, it also carries risks and challenges for mainstream adoption and stability.

Cryptocurrency plays a multifaceted role in the modern financial system, offering solutions to some of the most pressing challenges facing traditional banking models and providing new opportunities for financial inclusion, decentralization, and innovation. As cryptocurrency continues to evolve and mature, its impact on the global economy and financial landscape is likely to be profound, shaping the future of finance in ways we are only beginning to imagine. However, regulatory clarity, technological advancements, and broader acceptance will be crucial factors in determining the long-term viability and success of cryptocurrency in the modern financial system.

Chapter 3: The Mechanics of Blockchain

In this chapter, we'll delve into the intricate mechanics that power blockchain technology. From the fundamental components of a blockchain to the consensus mechanisms that ensure its integrity, we'll explore how blockchain operates at a technical level. Understanding these mechanics is essential for grasping the inner workings of blockchain and its applications across various industries.

1. Anatomy of a Blockchain

At its core, a blockchain is a distributed ledger that records transactions securely and transparently. Let's dissect the anatomy of a blockchain to understand its key components:

- **Blocks**: Blocks are containers that hold a collection of transactions. Each block contains a header and a list of transactions. The header includes metadata such as the block's hash, timestamp, and a reference to the previous block's hash, which creates the chain-like structure of the blockchain.
- **Transactions**: Transactions represent the transfer of value from one party to another. Each transaction contains details such as the sender's address, the recipient's address, and the amount of value being transferred.
- **Hash Functions**: Hash functions play a crucial role in blockchain by generating unique identifiers for blocks and transactions. These cryptographic hash functions ensure the integrity and immutability of the blockchain, as any change to the contents of a block would result in a different hash.

2. Consensus Mechanisms

Consensus mechanisms are protocols that enable nodes in a blockchain network to agree on the state of the blockchain. Let's explore some common consensus mechanisms:

- **Proof of Work (PoW)**: PoW is the original consensus mechanism used by Bitcoin. Miners compete to solve complex mathematical puzzles, and the first miner to find a valid solution is rewarded with newly minted bitcoins. PoW ensures that the majority of nodes agree on the validity of transactions and blocks.
- **Proof of Stake (PoS)**: In a PoS system, validators are selected to create new blocks based on the amount of cryptocurrency they hold and are willing to "stake" as collateral. PoS is more energy-efficient than PoW and promotes decentralization by rewarding participants with a stake in the network.
- **Delegated Proof of Stake (DPoS)**: DPoS is a variation of PoS where stakeholders vote to elect a set of delegates who are responsible for validating transactions and creating new blocks. DPoS aims to achieve scalability and efficiency by delegating decision-making authority to a smaller group of trusted nodes.

3. Mining and Network Security

Mining is the process by which new blocks are added to the blockchain, and transactions are validated. Let's explore the role of mining in maintaining network security:

- **Miners**: Miners use computational power to solve cryptographic puzzles and validate transactions. In return for their efforts, miners are rewarded with newly minted cryptocurrency and transaction fees.
- **Network Security**: Mining plays a crucial role in securing the blockchain network by preventing double-spending and other malicious activities. The computational power required to mine blocks makes it economically infeasible for attackers to manipulate the blockchain.

The mechanics of blockchain are intricate and multifaceted, involving a combination of cryptographic principles, consensus mechanisms, and network incentives. By understanding the inner workings of blockchain technology, we gain insight into its capabilities and limitations, as well as its potential to revolutionize industries ranging from finance and supply chain management to healthcare and governance. In the next chapter, we'll explore real-world applications of blockchain and the transformative impact it has on various sectors.

3.1. Decentralization: The Core Principle

Decentralization lies at the heart of blockchain technology, serving as its core principle and guiding ethos. In this section, we'll delve into the concept of decentralization and its significance in the context of blockchain.

Understanding Decentralization

- **Definition**: Decentralization refers to the distribution of power, authority, and control across a network of nodes, rather than concentrating it in a single central authority or entity. In the context of blockchain, decentralization entails removing the need for a central intermediary or trusted third party to validate transactions and maintain the integrity of the system.
- **Resilience**: Decentralization enhances the resilience of the blockchain network by eliminating single points of failure. Unlike centralized systems that are vulnerable to disruptions or attacks on a central authority, decentralized networks distribute control among numerous nodes, making them more robust and resistant to censorship or tampering.
- **Trustlessness**: Decentralization enables trustless transactions, meaning that participants can interact with each other and conduct transactions without the need for mutual trust or reliance on intermediaries. By leveraging cryptographic techniques and consensus mechanisms, decentralized networks achieve agreement and validation without the need for a trusted central authority.

Decentralization in Blockchain

- **Node Network**: In a blockchain network, nodes are distributed across geographically diverse locations, each maintaining a copy of the entire blockchain ledger. These nodes communicate with each other to validate transactions and ensure consensus on the state of the blockchain.
- **Removal of Intermediaries**: Blockchain eliminates the need for intermediaries such as banks, payment processors, or

clearinghouses by enabling peer-to-peer transactions directly between participants. Transactions are validated and recorded on the blockchain through consensus mechanisms, ensuring transparency and security without relying on a central authority.

- **Immutable Ledger**: The decentralized nature of blockchain ensures the immutability and integrity of the ledger. Once a transaction is validated and recorded on the blockchain, it becomes a permanent and tamper-proof record that cannot be altered or erased retroactively. This transparency and auditability enhance trust and accountability within the network.

Benefits of Decentralization

- **Enhanced Security**: Decentralization reduces the risk of attacks or manipulation by distributing control among numerous nodes. Even if a subset of nodes is compromised or malicious, the majority of honest nodes can maintain the integrity of the network.
- **Greater Privacy**: Decentralization promotes privacy by minimizing the collection and centralization of sensitive data. Participants retain control over their personal information and digital assets, reducing the risk of surveillance or unauthorized access.
- **Increased Freedom and Autonomy**: Decentralization empowers individuals and communities by providing greater autonomy and control over their financial assets, digital identities, and interactions within the network. Participants are not beholden to centralized authorities or intermediaries, enabling greater freedom of choice and self-determination.

Decentralization is the cornerstone of blockchain technology, enabling trustless transactions, enhancing security, and promoting freedom and autonomy. By distributing power and control across a network of nodes, blockchain achieves consensus and validation in a transparent and resilient manner, without relying on centralized authorities or intermediaries. Embracing decentralization opens up new possibilities for innovation, collaboration, and empowerment, shaping a future where individuals and communities have greater control over their digital destinies.

3.2. Cryptographic Hashing: Ensuring Security

Cryptographic hashing is a fundamental component of blockchain technology, playing a crucial role in ensuring the security and integrity of the blockchain. In this section, we'll explore the concept of cryptographic hashing and its significance in the context of blockchain.

Understanding Cryptographic Hashing

- **Definition**: Cryptographic hashing is a process that takes an input (or "message") and produces a fixed-size string of characters, known as a hash value or digest. This hash value is unique to the input data, and even a small change in the input results in a significantly different hash value. Cryptographic hash functions are one-way functions, meaning that it is computationally infeasible to reverse-engineer the original input from the hash value.
- **Properties**: Cryptographic hash functions possess several important properties, including:

- o **Deterministic**: For a given input, a cryptographic hash function always produces the same hash value.
- o **Fast Computation**: Hash functions can generate hash values quickly, making them suitable for real-time applications.
- o **Fixed Length**: Hash values have a fixed length, regardless of the size of the input data.
- o **Preimage Resistance**: It is computationally infeasible to find the original input from its hash value.
- o **Collision Resistance**: It is computationally infeasible to find two different inputs that produce the same hash value.

Application in Blockchain

- **Block Validation**: In blockchain, each block contains a header and a list of transactions. The header includes a hash value that uniquely identifies the block and references the hash value of the previous block, creating a chain-like structure. Any change to the contents of a block would result in a different hash value, thereby alerting the network to tampering attempts.
- **Transaction Integrity**: Cryptographic hashing ensures the integrity of transactions by creating a digital fingerprint of each transaction. This fingerprint is included in the block's hash value, providing a tamper-proof record of the transaction history. Even a small change to a transaction would result in a different hash value, making it easy to detect and reject invalid transactions.
- **Data Integrity**: Cryptographic hashing is used to verify the integrity of data stored on the blockchain. By calculating the hash value of a piece of data and comparing it to a known hash value, users can ensure that the data has not been altered or corrupted.

Benefits of Cryptographic Hashing

- **Security**: Cryptographic hashing provides a robust mechanism for ensuring the security and integrity of blockchain data. By creating unique and irreversible hash values for each piece of data, cryptographic hash functions prevent tampering, forgery, and unauthorized modifications.
- **Efficiency**: Hash functions are computationally efficient, allowing blockchain networks to generate hash values quickly and process transactions in real-time. This efficiency is essential for maintaining the scalability and responsiveness of blockchain systems, particularly in high-throughput environments.
- **Trustlessness**: Cryptographic hashing enables trustless transactions and interactions within the blockchain network. Participants can verify the integrity of data and transactions without relying on centralized authorities or intermediaries, enhancing transparency and accountability.

Cryptographic hashing is a foundational concept in blockchain technology, providing a robust mechanism for ensuring the security, integrity, and trustworthiness of blockchain data. By leveraging cryptographic hash functions, blockchain networks can create tamper-proof records of transactions, verify data integrity, and enable trustless interactions among participants. As blockchain technology continues to evolve and expand into new domains, cryptographic hashing will remain a critical tool for maintaining the security and reliability of decentralized systems.

3.3. Consensus Mechanisms: Proof of Work vs. Proof of Stake

Consensus mechanisms are essential components of blockchain technology, enabling decentralized networks to agree on the state of the blockchain and validate transactions. In this section, we'll compare two prominent consensus mechanisms: Proof of Work (PoW) and Proof of Stake (PoS).

1. Proof of Work (PoW)

- **Definition**: PoW is the original consensus mechanism used by Bitcoin and many other blockchain networks. In a PoW system, miners compete to solve complex mathematical puzzles, known as hash functions, using computational power. The first miner to find a valid solution is rewarded with newly minted cryptocurrency and transaction fees.
- **Security**: PoW ensures the security and integrity of the blockchain by requiring miners to invest computational resources in solving puzzles. This computational effort makes it economically infeasible for attackers to manipulate the blockchain, as they would need to control a majority of the network's computational power—a concept known as the 51% attack.
- **Energy Consumption**: One of the drawbacks of PoW is its high energy consumption. Mining requires significant computational power, leading to substantial electricity consumption and environmental concerns. Critics argue that PoW-based blockchain networks contribute to carbon emissions and energy wastage.

2. Proof of Stake (PoS)

- **Definition**: PoS is an alternative consensus mechanism that aims to address the energy inefficiency of PoW. In a PoS system, validators are selected to create new blocks and validate transactions based on the amount of cryptocurrency they hold and are willing to "stake" as collateral. Validators are rewarded with transaction fees and newly minted cryptocurrency.
- **Energy Efficiency**: PoS is more energy-efficient than PoW because it does not require miners to perform computationally intensive calculations. Instead, validators are chosen based on their stake in the network, reducing the energy consumption associated with block creation and validation.
- **Security**: PoS maintains security through economic incentives rather than computational power. Validators are financially incentivized to act honestly and validate transactions accurately, as they risk losing their staked cryptocurrency if they behave maliciously or validate fraudulent transactions.

3. Comparison

- **Energy Consumption**: PoS is generally considered more energy-efficient than PoW, as it does not rely on intensive computational calculations. This makes PoS an attractive option for blockchain networks seeking to reduce their environmental impact and energy costs.
- **Decentralization**: PoW is often praised for its decentralization, as it allows anyone with computational resources to participate in the network as a miner. In contrast, PoS may be criticized for favoring

wealthier participants who hold a larger stake in the network, potentially leading to centralization.

- **Security**: Both PoW and PoS mechanisms aim to ensure the security and integrity of the blockchain, albeit through different means. PoW relies on computational effort, while PoS relies on economic incentives. The effectiveness of each mechanism in maintaining security depends on factors such as network size, stake distribution, and attack vectors.

Proof of Work and Proof of Stake are two prominent consensus mechanisms used in blockchain technology, each with its advantages and drawbacks. While PoW has been the traditional choice for many blockchain networks, PoS offers a more energy-efficient alternative that may be better suited for certain use cases. As blockchain technology continues to evolve, consensus mechanisms will remain a critical area of innovation and experimentation, shaping the future of decentralized systems.

3.4. Smart Contracts: Automation on the Blockchain

Smart contracts represent a revolutionary application of blockchain technology, enabling automated and self-executing agreements without the need for intermediaries. In this section, we'll explore the concept of smart contracts and their transformative potential in various industries.

Understanding Smart Contracts

- **Definition**: Smart contracts are self-executing contracts with the terms of the agreement directly written into code. These contracts are stored and executed on a blockchain network, allowing for automated transactions and agreements between parties without the need for intermediaries.
- **Code as Law**: Smart contracts embody the principle of "code is law," meaning that the terms and conditions of the contract are enforced automatically by the underlying blockchain protocol. Once deployed, smart contracts execute predefined actions when specified conditions are met, providing trustless and tamper-proof execution of agreements.
- **Decentralized Execution**: Smart contracts are executed on a decentralized network of nodes, ensuring transparency, security, and immutability. Each transaction and contract execution is recorded on the blockchain, providing an auditable and tamper-proof record of events.

Applications of Smart Contracts

- **Financial Services**: Smart contracts have numerous applications in the financial services industry, including automated lending and borrowing, decentralized exchanges, and programmable insurance policies. These contracts enable secure and efficient financial transactions without the need for traditional intermediaries such as banks or insurance companies.
- **Supply Chain Management**: Smart contracts can streamline supply chain processes by automating the tracking and verification of goods as they move through the supply chain. By recording information such as product origin, shipping details, and quality

control measures on the blockchain, smart contracts enhance transparency, traceability, and accountability.

- **Legal and Governance**: Smart contracts have the potential to revolutionize legal and governance processes by automating the execution of legal agreements, property transfers, and voting procedures. These contracts can provide a transparent and immutable record of legal transactions, reducing the need for costly and time-consuming legal intermediaries.

Benefits of Smart Contracts

- **Efficiency**: Smart contracts automate repetitive tasks and eliminate the need for manual intervention, reducing the time and resources required to execute agreements. This efficiency leads to faster transaction processing, lower costs, and improved productivity across various industries.

- **Transparency**: Smart contracts operate on a decentralized network, providing transparency and visibility into contract terms, execution, and outcomes. Participants can verify the integrity of transactions and agreements without relying on centralized authorities or intermediaries.

- **Security**: Smart contracts are tamper-proof and resistant to fraud, thanks to their execution on a blockchain network. The cryptographic principles and consensus mechanisms underlying blockchain technology ensure the integrity and immutability of smart contract execution, reducing the risk of manipulation or unauthorized changes.

Challenges and Considerations

- **Complexity**: Developing and deploying smart contracts can be complex, requiring expertise in programming languages, cryptography, and blockchain technology. Additionally, smart contracts are immutable once deployed, making it essential to thoroughly audit and test the code to ensure its correctness and security.

- **Legal and Regulatory Compliance**: While smart contracts offer numerous benefits, they may raise legal and regulatory challenges related to contract enforceability, liability, and dispute resolution. As smart contract adoption grows, policymakers and legal experts will need to address these challenges to ensure compatibility with existing legal frameworks.

Smart contracts represent a groundbreaking application of blockchain technology, enabling automated and self-executing agreements across various industries. By leveraging cryptographic principles and decentralized networks, smart contracts offer efficiency, transparency, and security in the execution of agreements, while reducing reliance on traditional intermediaries. As smart contract adoption continues to grow, their transformative potential to streamline processes, enhance trust, and drive innovation is poised to reshape the future of commerce, governance, and beyond.

3.5. Privacy and Security in Blockchain

Privacy and security are paramount considerations in blockchain technology, as they determine the trustworthiness and integrity of the decentralized network. In this section, we'll explore the mechanisms and challenges associated with privacy and security in blockchain.

Privacy in Blockchain

- **Pseudonymity**: Blockchain offers pseudonymous transactions, meaning that users are identified by cryptographic addresses rather than personal information. While this provides a degree of privacy, it does not guarantee anonymity, as transactions are recorded on a public ledger that can be analyzed and traced.

- **Privacy Coins**: Some blockchain networks, such as Monero and Zcash, specialize in privacy-enhancing features that obfuscate transaction details, sender and recipient addresses, and transaction amounts. These privacy coins offer enhanced privacy and anonymity for users seeking greater confidentiality in their transactions.

- **Zero-Knowledge Proofs**: Zero-knowledge proofs are cryptographic techniques that enable a prover to demonstrate knowledge of a secret without revealing the secret itself. These proofs can be used to validate transactions without disclosing sensitive information, providing privacy-preserving solutions for blockchain applications.

Security in Blockchain

- **Cryptography**: Blockchain relies on cryptographic techniques such as hashing, digital signatures, and encryption to secure transactions and data. These cryptographic primitives ensure the integrity, authenticity, and confidentiality of information stored on the blockchain, protecting it from tampering and unauthorized access.
- **Consensus Mechanisms**: Consensus mechanisms such as Proof of Work (PoW) and Proof of Stake (PoS) ensure the security and immutability of the blockchain by preventing double-spending and malicious attacks. These mechanisms incentivize participants to act honestly and validate transactions accurately, maintaining the integrity of the network.
- **Immutable Ledger**: The immutable nature of the blockchain ledger ensures that once a transaction is recorded, it cannot be altered or deleted retroactively. This tamper-proof record provides a transparent and auditable history of transactions, enhancing accountability and trust within the network.

Challenges and Considerations

- **Scalability vs. Privacy**: Achieving both scalability and privacy in blockchain networks remains a significant challenge. Privacy-enhancing features such as zero-knowledge proofs may introduce computational overhead and complexity, impacting the scalability and performance of the network.
- **Regulatory Compliance**: Privacy features in blockchain may raise concerns among regulators and policymakers, particularly in industries with stringent regulatory requirements such as finance

and healthcare. Balancing privacy with regulatory compliance poses challenges for blockchain adoption and integration into existing legal frameworks.

- **Cybersecurity Risks**: Blockchain networks are not immune to cybersecurity risks such as hacking, phishing attacks, and malware. While blockchain offers robust cryptographic security, vulnerabilities in smart contracts, wallet software, and network infrastructure can still be exploited by malicious actors, highlighting the importance of robust cybersecurity measures.

Privacy and security are foundational principles in blockchain technology, underpinning trust, integrity, and decentralization. By leveraging cryptographic techniques, consensus mechanisms, and privacy-enhancing features, blockchain networks can provide confidentiality, authenticity, and resilience in the face of cyber threats and privacy concerns. As blockchain technology continues to evolve and mature, addressing the challenges of privacy and security will be essential to realizing its full potential in transforming industries, safeguarding digital assets, and empowering individuals in the digital age.

Chapter 4: Blockchain Applications beyond Cryptocurrency

In this chapter, we'll explore the wide-ranging applications of blockchain technology beyond cryptocurrency. While cryptocurrency remains one of the most well-known uses of blockchain, its potential extends far beyond digital currencies. From supply chain management to healthcare and beyond, blockchain is revolutionizing industries by offering transparent, secure, and decentralized solutions to various challenges.

1. Supply Chain Management

Blockchain technology has the potential to transform supply chain management by providing transparency, traceability, and efficiency throughout the entire supply chain process. Here are some key applications:

- **Traceability**: Blockchain enables end-to-end traceability of products, allowing stakeholders to track the movement and origin of goods from the point of origin to the end consumer. This transparency helps prevent fraud, counterfeiting, and the distribution of counterfeit products.
- **Smart Contracts**: Smart contracts automate and enforce agreements between parties involved in the supply chain, such as manufacturers, suppliers, distributors, and retailers. These self-executing contracts streamline processes such as payment settlements, inventory management, and compliance with contractual obligations.

- **Product Authentication**: Blockchain can be used to verify the authenticity and integrity of products by recording unique identifiers, such as serial numbers or RFID tags, on the blockchain. This ensures that products are genuine and have not been tampered with throughout the supply chain.

2. Healthcare

Blockchain technology has the potential to revolutionize the healthcare industry by improving data security, interoperability, and patient outcomes. Here are some key applications:

- **Medical Records Management**: Blockchain enables secure and interoperable storage of medical records, allowing patients and healthcare providers to access and share health information seamlessly while maintaining patient privacy and data security.
- **Clinical Trials and Research**: Blockchain facilitates the secure and transparent sharing of clinical trial data, accelerating the research and development of new treatments and therapies. Smart contracts can automate the execution of research agreements and ensure compliance with regulatory requirements.
- **Drug Traceability**: Blockchain can be used to track the provenance and distribution of pharmaceutical drugs, reducing the risk of counterfeit medications entering the market and ensuring patient safety.

3. Voting and Governance

Blockchain technology offers transparent, tamper-proof, and auditable voting systems, enhancing the integrity and security of democratic processes. Here are some key applications:

- **Secure Voting Systems**: Blockchain-based voting systems enable secure and verifiable voting processes, allowing voters to cast their ballots anonymously while ensuring the integrity and transparency of election results.
- **Decentralized Governance**: Blockchain can facilitate decentralized decision-making processes by enabling transparent and auditable governance mechanisms. Decentralized autonomous organizations (DAOs) use blockchain-based smart contracts to automate governance processes and allocate resources based on consensus among stakeholders.
- **Anti-Corruption Measures**: Blockchain provides a tamper-proof record of transactions and decisions, reducing the risk of corruption and fraud in government and corporate governance.

Blockchain technology offers transformative solutions across various industries, extending far beyond cryptocurrency. From supply chain management to healthcare, voting, and governance, blockchain applications are revolutionizing traditional processes by providing transparency, security, and efficiency. As blockchain continues to evolve and mature, its potential to drive innovation, streamline operations, and empower individuals and organizations will only continue to grow.

4.1. Blockchain in Finance: Beyond Bitcoin

While Bitcoin introduced the world to blockchain technology, its applications in finance extend far beyond cryptocurrency. In this section, we'll explore how blockchain is revolutionizing the financial industry by offering transparent, secure, and efficient solutions to traditional banking and financial services.

1. Payment and Remittance

Cross-Border Payments: Blockchain enables fast, low-cost, and secure cross-border payments by eliminating the need for intermediaries such as banks and payment processors. Cryptocurrencies and stablecoins can be transferred directly between parties across borders, reducing transaction fees and settlement times.

Remittances: Blockchain-based remittance platforms offer an alternative to traditional money transfer services, allowing individuals to send funds internationally at a fraction of the cost and time associated with traditional remittance methods. These platforms leverage blockchain technology to streamline the remittance process and increase financial inclusion for underserved populations.

2. Clearing and Settlement

Real-Time Settlement: Blockchain facilitates real-time clearing and settlement of financial transactions by providing a transparent and immutable ledger of transactions. Smart contracts automate settlement processes, reducing counterparty risk and eliminating the need for intermediaries such as clearinghouses and custodians.

Securities Settlement: Blockchain technology has the potential to streamline securities settlement processes by enabling peer-to-peer trading and ownership transfer of securities. Asset-backed tokens represent ownership of securities such as stocks, bonds, and commodities, allowing for instant settlement and increased liquidity in capital markets.

3. Trade Finance and Supply Chain Financing

Trade Finance: Blockchain streamlines trade finance processes such as letter of credit issuance, invoice financing, and trade documentation management by providing a transparent and secure platform for trade-related transactions. Smart contracts automate and enforce agreements between parties, reducing paperwork, delays, and costs associated with traditional trade finance methods.

Supply Chain Financing: Blockchain enables supply chain financing solutions that provide access to liquidity for suppliers and manufacturers by leveraging supply chain data as collateral. By recording transaction and shipment details on the blockchain, lenders can assess the creditworthiness of borrowers and offer financing based on verifiable supply chain information.

4. Identity Verification and KYC

- **Identity Verification**: Blockchain-based identity verification solutions offer secure and decentralized methods for verifying individuals' identities, reducing the risk of identity theft and fraud. Self-sovereign identity systems empower individuals to control and share their personal information securely, enhancing privacy and security in identity management.

- **KYC (Know Your Customer)**: Blockchain streamlines KYC processes by providing a shared and immutable record of customer identity verification data. Financial institutions can access verified KYC information securely and efficiently, reducing duplication of efforts and enhancing compliance with regulatory requirements.

Blockchain technology is reshaping the financial industry by offering innovative solutions that improve efficiency, transparency, and security in banking and financial services. From payment and remittance to clearing and settlement, trade finance, and identity verification, blockchain applications in finance extend far beyond Bitcoin and cryptocurrencies. As blockchain adoption continues to grow, financial institutions, regulators, and consumers alike stand to benefit from the transformative potential of this revolutionary technology.

4.2. Blockchain in Supply Chain Management

Blockchain technology is revolutionizing supply chain management by providing transparency, traceability, and efficiency throughout the entire supply chain process. In this section, we'll explore how blockchain is transforming supply chain management and enhancing trust and accountability among stakeholders.

1. Traceability and Transparency

- **End-to-end Traceability**: Blockchain enables end-to-end traceability of products, allowing stakeholders to track the movement and origin of goods from the point of origin to the end consumer. Each transaction and event in the supply chain, such as production, shipping, and delivery, is recorded on the blockchain, providing a transparent and auditable record of the product's journey.
- **Supply Chain Visibility**: Blockchain provides real-time visibility into supply chain operations by sharing information across all participants in the network. This transparency allows stakeholders to identify inefficiencies, bottlenecks, and areas for improvement in the supply chain process, leading to better decision-making and resource allocation.

2. Fraud Prevention and Counterfeiting

- **Fraud Prevention**: Blockchain reduces the risk of fraud and counterfeit products entering the supply chain by providing a tamper-proof record of transactions and product authenticity. Each product is assigned a unique identifier, such as a serial number or RFID tag, which is recorded on the blockchain. Any attempt to tamper with or counterfeit the product can be detected and traced back to its source.
- **Product Authentication**: Blockchain enables consumers to verify the authenticity and integrity of products by scanning a QR code or NFC tag on the product packaging. This authentication process provides consumers with confidence that the product they are purchasing is genuine and has not been tampered with during transit.

3. Supply Chain Financing

- **Streamlined Financing**: Blockchain streamlines supply chain financing processes by providing a transparent and immutable record of transactions and asset ownership. Smart contracts automate and enforce agreements between suppliers, manufacturers, and financiers, reducing paperwork, delays, and costs associated with traditional financing methods.
- **Risk Mitigation**: Blockchain mitigates the risk of supply chain financing by providing lenders with access to verifiable supply chain data as collateral. This data includes transaction and shipment details recorded on the blockchain, allowing lenders to assess the creditworthiness of borrowers and make informed lending decisions.

4. Sustainability and Ethical Sourcing

- **Ethical Sourcing**: Blockchain promotes ethical sourcing practices by providing transparency into the origin and production process of goods. Consumers can verify that products are sourced from ethical and sustainable suppliers, ensuring compliance with labor standards, environmental regulations, and fair trade practices.
- **Carbon Footprint Reduction**: Blockchain reduces the carbon footprint of supply chains by optimizing logistics and transportation routes, reducing waste and emissions associated with inefficient supply chain practices. Smart contracts automate and optimize supply chain processes, leading to more sustainable and environmentally friendly operations.

Blockchain technology is transforming supply chain management by providing transparency, traceability, and efficiency across the entire supply chain process. From traceability and transparency to fraud prevention, supply chain financing, and sustainability, blockchain applications in supply chain management offer innovative solutions to traditional challenges. As blockchain adoption continues to grow, businesses, consumers, and stakeholders across industries stand to benefit from the increased trust, accountability, and efficiency enabled by blockchain technology.

4.3. Healthcare and Blockchain: Ensuring Data Integrity

Blockchain technology holds immense promise for transforming the healthcare industry by improving data integrity, interoperability, and patient outcomes. In this section, we'll explore how blockchain is revolutionizing healthcare by providing secure and transparent solutions for data management and patient care.

1. Electronic Health Records (EHRs)

- **Secure and Interoperable EHRs**: Blockchain enables secure and interoperable storage of electronic health records (EHRs) by providing a decentralized and immutable ledger of patient health information. Each patient's medical records are encrypted and stored on the blockchain, allowing authorized healthcare providers to access and update the records securely and efficiently.
- **Patient Control and Consent**: Blockchain empowers patients to control and manage their health data by granting or revoking access to their EHRs via cryptographic keys. Patients can

selectively share their health information with healthcare providers, researchers, and other authorized entities, ensuring privacy and confidentiality.

2. Clinical Trials and Research

- **Transparent and Auditable Clinical Trials**: Blockchain facilitates transparent and auditable clinical trials by providing a tamper-proof record of trial data, including patient recruitment, informed consent, and trial outcomes. Smart contracts automate and enforce agreements between trial participants, investigators, and sponsors, ensuring compliance with regulatory requirements and ethical standards.
- **Data Sharing and Collaboration**: Blockchain enables secure and transparent sharing of research data among stakeholders, including researchers, institutions, and pharmaceutical companies. Researchers can access and analyze anonymized patient data stored on the blockchain, leading to collaborative research efforts and accelerated discovery of new treatments and therapies.

3. Drug Traceability and Supply Chain Management

- **Secure Drug Traceability**: Blockchain enhances drug traceability and supply chain management by providing a transparent and immutable record of pharmaceutical products from manufacturing to distribution. Each transaction and shipment of drugs is recorded on the blockchain, allowing stakeholders to verify the authenticity and integrity of drugs and prevent counterfeit medications from entering the market.

- **Efficient Supply Chain Management**: Blockchain streamlines supply chain management processes by automating and optimizing logistics, inventory management, and procurement. Smart contracts automate and enforce agreements between suppliers, manufacturers, and distributors, reducing paperwork, delays, and costs associated with traditional supply chain methods.

4. Data Security and Privacy

- **Immutable Data Integrity**: Blockchain ensures the integrity and security of healthcare data by providing a tamper-proof and auditable record of transactions and patient information. Once recorded on the blockchain, healthcare data cannot be altered or deleted retroactively, providing a secure and reliable source of truth for medical records and transactions.
- **Enhanced Privacy Protection**: Blockchain enhances privacy protection by encrypting patient health information and providing granular control over data access and sharing. Patients can grant permission for specific healthcare providers or researchers to access their data securely while maintaining confidentiality and compliance with privacy regulations such as HIPAA.

Blockchain technology is poised to revolutionize the healthcare industry by providing secure, transparent, and efficient solutions for data management, patient care, and research. From electronic health records and clinical trials to drug traceability and data security, blockchain applications in healthcare offer transformative benefits that improve outcomes for patients, providers, and stakeholders. As blockchain adoption continues to grow, the healthcare industry stands to benefit from increased trust, interoperability, and innovation enabled by blockchain technology.

4.4. Blockchain for Digital Identity Verification

Blockchain technology is reshaping digital identity verification by providing secure, decentralized, and tamper-proof solutions for identity management. In this section, we'll explore how blockchain is revolutionizing digital identity verification and enhancing privacy, security, and trust in online interactions.

1. Self-Sovereign Identity

- **Ownership and Control**: Blockchain enables self-sovereign identity, where individuals have ownership and control over their own digital identities. Rather than relying on centralized identity providers or government-issued credentials, individuals manage their identity information using cryptographic keys stored on the blockchain.
- **Privacy Protection**: Self-sovereign identity empowers individuals to selectively share their identity information with trusted parties while maintaining privacy and confidentiality. Users can authenticate themselves without revealing unnecessary personal data, reducing the risk of identity theft, fraud, and surveillance.

2. Immutable Identity Records

- **Tamper-Proof Records**: Blockchain provides a tamper-proof and immutable record of identity-related transactions and credentials. Each identity verification event, such as the issuance of a digital ID or the authentication of a user, is recorded on the blockchain, ensuring the integrity and authenticity of identity records.
- **Auditability and Transparency**: Blockchain enables auditable and transparent identity verification processes by providing a transparent ledger of identity-related transactions. Authorized parties, such as employers, government agencies, and financial institutions, can verify the authenticity of identity credentials by accessing the blockchain record.

3. Decentralized Authentication

- **Secure Authentication**: Blockchain facilitates secure and decentralized authentication mechanisms, allowing users to prove their identity without relying on centralized authorities or intermediaries. Decentralized identity platforms use cryptographic techniques such as digital signatures and zero-knowledge proofs to verify the authenticity of identity claims without exposing sensitive information.
- **Interoperability**: Decentralized identity solutions promote interoperability by enabling seamless authentication across different platforms and services. Users can use their digital identities to access a wide range of applications, websites, and services without the need to create and manage multiple accounts and passwords.

4. Use Cases and Applications

- **Financial Services**: Blockchain-based digital identity solutions enhance Know Your Customer (KYC) and Anti-Money Laundering (AML) compliance for financial institutions by providing secure and verifiable identity verification processes.
- **Healthcare**: Blockchain enables secure and interoperable sharing of patient health information among healthcare providers, improving care coordination and patient outcomes while maintaining privacy and confidentiality.
- **E-Government**: Blockchain facilitates secure and transparent e-government services, such as voting, land registry, and identity management, by providing tamper-proof records of citizen identities and transactions.

Blockchain technology is revolutionizing digital identity verification by providing secure, decentralized, and privacy-enhancing solutions for identity management. From self-sovereign identity and immutable identity records to decentralized authentication and interoperability, blockchain applications in digital identity offer transformative benefits that enhance privacy, security, and trust in online interactions. As blockchain adoption continues to grow, individuals, organizations, and governments alike stand to benefit from the increased control, transparency, and efficiency enabled by blockchain-based digital identity solutions.

4.5. Emerging Applications and Future Trends

The potential of blockchain technology extends far beyond its current applications, with emerging use cases and future trends poised to revolutionize various industries. In this section, we'll explore some of the emerging applications and trends shaping the future of blockchain technology.

1. Decentralized Finance (DeFi)

- **Decentralized Exchanges**: Decentralized finance (DeFi) platforms enable peer-to-peer trading of digital assets without the need for traditional intermediaries such as banks or exchanges. Decentralized exchanges (DEXs) leverage blockchain technology to provide transparent, secure, and permissionless trading of cryptocurrencies and tokens.
- **Lending and Borrowing**: DeFi protocols facilitate decentralized lending and borrowing of digital assets, allowing users to earn interest on their idle assets or borrow funds against collateral without relying on traditional financial institutions. Smart contracts automate and enforce lending agreements, reducing counterparty risk and increasing access to capital for individuals and businesses.

2. Non-Fungible Tokens (NFTs)

- **Digital Ownership and Collectibles**: Non-fungible tokens (NFTs) represent unique digital assets, such as art, music, video games, and virtual real estate, on the blockchain. NFTs enable digital ownership and provenance tracking of digital content, allowing creators to monetize their work and collectors to buy, sell, and trade unique digital collectibles securely and transparently.

- **Tokenization of Real-World Assets**: NFTs can also represent ownership of real-world assets, such as real estate, luxury goods, and intellectual property rights. Tokenizing real-world assets on the blockchain enables fractional ownership, liquidity, and transparent transfer of assets, unlocking new investment opportunities and increasing accessibility to asset classes traditionally inaccessible to retail investors.

3. Blockchain Interoperability and Scalability

- **Interoperability Protocols**: Blockchain interoperability protocols enable seamless communication and transfer of assets and data across different blockchain networks. Interoperability solutions such as cross-chain bridges, sidechains, and interoperability standards facilitate interoperability between disparate blockchain ecosystems, promoting collaboration, innovation, and adoption across the blockchain space.
- **Scalability Solutions**: Scalability remains a critical challenge for blockchain adoption, particularly in high-throughput applications such as payments, gaming, and decentralized finance. Scalability solutions such as layer 2 scaling solutions, sharding, and consensus protocol optimizations aim to increase the transaction throughput and reduce the latency of blockchain networks, enabling mass adoption and mainstream usage.

4. Privacy-Preserving Technologies

- **Zero-Knowledge Proofs**: Zero-knowledge proofs (ZKPs) are cryptographic techniques that enable parties to prove the validity of a statement without revealing any sensitive information. ZKPs enhance privacy and confidentiality in blockchain transactions by allowing users to authenticate themselves or verify the integrity of data without disclosing unnecessary details, reducing the risk of privacy breaches and unauthorized access.

- **Privacy Coins and Confidential Transactions**: Privacy-focused cryptocurrencies and protocols incorporate privacy-enhancing features such as confidential transactions, ring signatures, and stealth addresses to obfuscate transaction details and protect user privacy. Privacy coins such as Monero, Zcash, and Dash offer enhanced privacy and anonymity for users seeking confidentiality in their transactions.

The future of blockchain technology is bright, with emerging applications and trends poised to revolutionize various industries and reshape the digital landscape. From decentralized finance (DeFi) and non-fungible tokens (NFTs) to blockchain interoperability, scalability solutions, and privacy-preserving technologies, blockchain innovations are unlocking new opportunities for decentralization, transparency, and trust in the digital economy. As blockchain adoption continues to accelerate, the potential for transformative impact across industries and society as a whole is boundless, paving the way for a more inclusive, transparent, and decentralized future.

Chapter 5: Investing in Blockchain and Cryptocurrencies

In this chapter, we'll explore the opportunities and considerations for investing in blockchain technology and cryptocurrencies. From understanding the fundamentals of blockchain to navigating the volatile cryptocurrency markets, we'll delve into the strategies and best practices for investors looking to capitalize on the potential of this emerging asset class.

1. Understanding Blockchain Fundamentals

- **Fundamental Concepts**: Before investing in blockchain and cryptocurrencies, it's essential to understand the fundamental concepts of blockchain technology, including decentralization, consensus mechanisms, cryptographic security, and smart contracts. A solid grasp of these concepts will help investors assess the potential of blockchain projects and make informed investment decisions.

- **Industry Applications**: Investors should research and analyze the various industry applications of blockchain technology, including finance, supply chain management, healthcare, and decentralized applications (dApps). Understanding the potential use cases and market demand for blockchain solutions can help investors identify promising investment opportunities.

2. Investing in Cryptocurrencies

- **Diversification**: Diversification is key to managing risk in cryptocurrency investments. Investors should diversify their cryptocurrency holdings across different assets, such as Bitcoin, Ethereum, and altcoins, to mitigate the impact of market volatility and reduce exposure to individual asset risks.
- **Research and Due Diligence**: Thorough research and due diligence are essential when investing in cryptocurrencies. Investors should evaluate factors such as project fundamentals, team expertise, technology innovation, market demand, and competitive landscape before allocating capital to specific cryptocurrencies.
- **Risk Management**: Cryptocurrency investments carry inherent risks, including price volatility, regulatory uncertainty, cybersecurity threats, and market manipulation. Investors should establish risk management strategies, such as setting stop-loss orders, diversifying their portfolios, and allocating only a portion of their investment capital to cryptocurrencies.

3. Investing in Blockchain Stocks and Companies

- **Publicly Traded Companies**: Investors can gain exposure to blockchain technology through publicly traded companies that are leveraging blockchain for various applications, such as financial services, supply chain management, and technology infrastructure. Researching and analyzing the business models, revenue streams, and competitive advantages of blockchain companies can help investors identify investment opportunities in the stock market.

- **Blockchain ETFs and Funds**: Exchange-traded funds (ETFs) and mutual funds focused on blockchain and cryptocurrency-related companies offer diversified exposure to the blockchain industry. Investors can invest in blockchain ETFs and funds to gain exposure to a basket of blockchain stocks and companies, reducing individual company risk and volatility.

4. Regulatory and Market Considerations

- **Regulatory Landscape**: The regulatory landscape for blockchain and cryptocurrencies varies by jurisdiction and is subject to change. Investors should stay informed about regulatory developments, compliance requirements, and legal considerations related to cryptocurrency investments to mitigate regulatory risks and ensure compliance with applicable laws.
- **Market Volatility**: Cryptocurrency markets are highly volatile and subject to significant price fluctuations. Investors should be prepared for price volatility and market uncertainty when investing in cryptocurrencies, and adopt a long-term investment horizon to weather short-term market fluctuations.

By understanding the fundamentals of blockchain technology, conducting thorough research and due diligence, diversifying their portfolios, and managing risks effectively, investors can capitalize on the potential of blockchain and cryptocurrencies to generate long-term returns and build wealth in the digital economy. As blockchain adoption continues to accelerate and mature, the opportunities for investment and growth in this space are boundless, making it an exciting and dynamic asset class for investors to explore.

5.1. The Basics of Cryptocurrency Investment

Investing in cryptocurrencies can be both exciting and rewarding, but it's essential to understand the basics before diving into this volatile market. In this section, we'll explore the fundamental principles of cryptocurrency investment to help you make informed decisions and navigate the complex world of digital assets.

1. Understanding Cryptocurrencies

- **Digital Assets**: Cryptocurrencies are digital or virtual currencies that utilize cryptography for secure transactions and control the creation of new units. Unlike traditional currencies issued by governments, cryptocurrencies operate on decentralized networks based on blockchain technology.
- **Decentralization**: Cryptocurrencies operate on decentralized networks, meaning they are not controlled by any single authority, such as a government or central bank. Instead, transactions are verified and recorded on a distributed ledger called the blockchain, which is maintained by a network of nodes.

2. Risk Management

- **Volatility**: Cryptocurrency markets are known for their high volatility, with prices often experiencing significant fluctuations in short periods. It's essential to be prepared for price swings and potential losses when investing in cryptocurrencies and to only invest what you can afford to lose.

- **Diversification**: Diversifying your cryptocurrency portfolio can help spread risk and reduce exposure to individual assets. Consider investing in a mix of established cryptocurrencies like Bitcoin and Ethereum, as well as promising altcoins with potential for growth.

3. Research and Due Diligence

- **Project Fundamentals**: Before investing in a cryptocurrency, research the project's fundamentals, including its use case, technology, team, community support, and market potential. Look for projects with clear objectives, strong development teams, and active communities.
- **Market Analysis**: Stay informed about market trends, news, and developments in the cryptocurrency space. Monitor price movements, trading volumes, and market sentiment to identify potential investment opportunities and make informed decisions.

4. Long-Term Perspective

- **Investment Horizon**: Cryptocurrency investment is often best approached with a long-term perspective. While short-term trading strategies can be lucrative, they also carry higher risk due to market volatility. Consider adopting a buy-and-hold strategy for long-term investment success.
- **Hodl Mentality**: The term "hodl" originated from a misspelling of "hold" and has become synonymous with the strategy of holding onto cryptocurrencies despite short-term price fluctuations. Embracing a hodl mentality can help investors weather market downturns and capitalize on long-term growth opportunities.

Investing in cryptocurrencies offers exciting opportunities for growth and profit, but it's essential to approach this market with caution and diligence. By understanding the basics of cryptocurrency investment, managing risks effectively, conducting thorough research, and maintaining a long-term perspective, investors can navigate the complexities of the cryptocurrency market and build a successful investment portfolio. As the cryptocurrency ecosystem continues to evolve and mature, the potential for investment opportunities and wealth creation in this space remains vast, making it an attractive asset class for investors seeking high-risk, high-reward opportunities.

5.2. Different Types of Crypto Assets: Coins, Tokens, and NFTs

The world of cryptocurrencies is diverse and multifaceted, comprising various types of digital assets. Understanding the differences between coins, tokens, and non-fungible tokens (NFTs) is crucial for making informed investment decisions. In this section, we'll explore these different types of crypto assets, their unique characteristics, and their roles in the digital economy.

1. Coins

- **Definition**: Coins are digital currencies that operate on their independent blockchain. They are designed primarily as a medium of exchange, store of value, or unit of account.
- **Examples**: The most well-known example of a coin is Bitcoin (BTC), the first cryptocurrency and the largest by market capitalization. Other prominent coins include Ethereum (ETH),

which powers the Ethereum blockchain, and Litecoin (LTC), known for its faster transaction times compared to Bitcoin.

- **Functions**: Coins are used for various purposes, including:

  - **Payments**: Facilitating transactions between parties for goods and services.
  - **Transfers**: Enabling the transfer of value across borders without intermediaries.
  - **Investment**: Serving as a digital asset for long-term holding and speculation.

2. Tokens

Definition: Tokens are digital assets that are created and managed on existing blockchain platforms, such as Ethereum. Unlike coins, tokens do not have their independent blockchain and rely on the infrastructure of the underlying blockchain.

- **Types of Tokens:**

  - **Utility Tokens**: Provide access to a specific product or service within a blockchain ecosystem. Examples include Binance Coin (BNB), which offers discounted trading fees on the Binance exchange, and Filecoin (FIL), used to access decentralized storage services.
  - **Security Tokens**: Represent ownership in an asset, such as equity, debt, or real estate. These tokens are subject to regulatory oversight and must comply with securities laws.

- o **Governance Tokens**: Grant holders the right to participate in the decision-making process of a blockchain project or decentralized autonomous organization (DAO). Examples include Maker (MKR) and Uniswap (UNI).

- **Functions**: Tokens have a wide range of applications, including:

  - o **Access**: Providing access to decentralized applications (dApps) and services.
  - o **Governance**: Allowing token holders to vote on project developments and protocol changes.
  - o **Investment**: Acting as investment vehicles representing fractional ownership in assets.

3. Non-Fungible Tokens (NFTs)

- **Definition**: NFTs are unique digital assets that represent ownership or proof of authenticity of a specific item or piece of content, such as art, music, collectibles, or virtual real estate. Each NFT is distinct and cannot be exchanged on a one-to-one basis with another NFT, making them non-fungible.
- **Examples**: Popular NFT projects include CryptoPunks, a collection of 10,000 unique 8-bit characters, and Bored Ape Yacht Club, a series of cartoon ape NFTs. NFTs are also used in the gaming industry, such as Axie Infinity, where players own and trade unique in-game assets.
- **Functions**: NFTs serve various purposes, including:

- **Digital Art and Collectibles**: Allowing artists and creators to tokenize their work and sell it directly to collectors, with verifiable ownership and provenance.
- **Virtual Real Estate**: Enabling ownership and trade of virtual land and properties within digital worlds, such as Decentraland and The Sandbox.
- **In-Game Assets**: Facilitating the ownership and trade of unique items within blockchain-based games.

The cryptocurrency ecosystem encompasses a wide variety of digital assets, each with its unique characteristics and use cases. Coins, tokens, and NFTs represent different facets of the digital economy, offering diverse opportunities for investment and innovation. By understanding the distinctions between these types of crypto assets, investors can make more informed decisions and capitalize on the evolving landscape of blockchain technology and digital assets. As the market continues to grow and mature, the potential for new and innovative applications of these assets remains vast, driving the ongoing expansion of the cryptocurrency space.

5.3. Cryptocurrency Exchanges: How to Buy and Trade

Cryptocurrency exchanges are platforms that facilitate the buying, selling, and trading of digital assets. Understanding how these exchanges work and how to use them effectively is crucial for any cryptocurrency investor. In this section, we'll explore the types of cryptocurrency exchanges, how to set up an account, and the process of buying and trading cryptocurrencies.

1. Types of Cryptocurrency Exchanges

Centralized Exchanges (CEXs):

- **Overview**: Centralized exchanges are run by companies that act as intermediaries between buyers and sellers. They offer a wide range of services, including fiat-to-crypto trading, advanced trading features, and customer support.
- **Examples**: Binance, Coinbase, Kraken, and Bitfinex.
- **Pros**: High liquidity, user-friendly interfaces, a wide range of supported cryptocurrencies, and robust security measures.
- **Cons**: Users must trust the exchange to hold their funds securely, and there is a higher risk of hacking and regulatory scrutiny.

Decentralized Exchanges (DEXs):

- **Overview**: Decentralized exchanges operate without a central authority, allowing peer-to-peer trading directly between users. They use smart contracts to facilitate transactions on the blockchain.
- **Examples**: Uniswap, SushiSwap, PancakeSwap, and Balancer.
- **Pros**: Greater privacy, control over funds, reduced risk of hacking, and no need for account verification.
- **Cons**: Lower liquidity compared to CEXs, potentially higher transaction fees, and a steeper learning curve for new users.

2. Setting Up an Account

Choose an Exchange: Research and select a reputable exchange based on factors such as security, fees, supported cryptocurrencies, and user reviews.

- **Account Registration:**

  - **Personal Information**: Provide your email address, create a strong password, and complete the registration process.
  - **Verification**: Many centralized exchanges require identity verification (KYC) to comply with regulatory requirements. This typically involves submitting a government-issued ID and proof of address.

- **Two-Factor Authentication (2FA)**: Enable 2FA to enhance the security of your account. This adds an extra layer of protection by requiring a second form of authentication, such as a code sent to your mobile device.

3. Depositing Funds

- **Fiat Deposits**: Link your bank account or credit card to deposit fiat currency (e.g., USD, EUR) into your exchange account. This process may take a few days, depending on the exchange and payment method.

- **Crypto Deposits**: If you already own cryptocurrency, you can deposit it into your exchange wallet. Navigate to the deposit section, select the cryptocurrency you want to deposit, and generate a wallet address. Transfer the funds from your external wallet to the provided address.

4. Buying and Trading Cryptocurrencies

Placing a Buy Order:

- **Market Order**: A market order executes immediately at the current market price. This is the fastest way to buy cryptocurrency, but you may not get the best possible price.
- **Limit Order**: A limit order allows you to set a specific price at which you want to buy. The order will only execute if the market reaches your specified price, giving you more control over the transaction.
- **Trading Pairs**: Exchanges offer various trading pairs, which are combinations of two different assets that can be traded against each other (e.g., BTC/USD, ETH/BTC). Choose the appropriate trading pair based on the cryptocurrency you want to buy or sell.

Executing a Trade:

- **Analyze the Market**: Use technical analysis tools and market indicators to inform your trading decisions.
- **Enter the Trade**: Once you've decided on a trade, enter the details into the exchange's trading interface and submit your order.

- **Monitor and Manage**: After placing a trade, monitor the market and manage your position as needed. You may want to set stop-loss and take-profit orders to automate your trading strategy.

5. Security and Best Practices

- **Secure Your Funds**: After purchasing cryptocurrencies, consider transferring them to a secure wallet (hardware or software) rather than leaving them on the exchange. This reduces the risk of losing funds in case the exchange is hacked.
- **Regular Updates**: Keep your exchange account and wallet software up to date to protect against security vulnerabilities.
- **Beware of Scams**: Be cautious of phishing attacks, fake exchanges, and other scams. Always verify the authenticity of the website and use official apps and software.

Cryptocurrency exchanges play a vital role in the digital asset ecosystem, providing a platform for buying, selling, and trading cryptocurrencies. By understanding the different types of exchanges, setting up and securing your account, and following best practices for trading, you can navigate the cryptocurrency markets effectively and make informed investment decisions. As the industry evolves, staying informed and adapting to new developments will be key to successfully managing your cryptocurrency investments.

5.4. Risks and Rewards: What Investors Need to Know

Investing in cryptocurrencies and blockchain technology offers substantial rewards but comes with significant risks. Understanding these risks and rewards is crucial for making informed investment decisions and managing your portfolio effectively. In this section, we'll explore the potential gains and dangers associated with investing in this volatile and rapidly evolving market.

Rewards of Cryptocurrency Investment

- **High Returns**: Cryptocurrencies have the potential for substantial returns. Bitcoin, for example, has seen exponential growth since its inception, rewarding early investors with significant profits. Altcoins can also provide high returns, especially during bull markets.
- **Diversification**: Cryptocurrencies offer a new asset class that can diversify traditional investment portfolios. Including digital assets in a portfolio can reduce overall risk through uncorrelated returns with traditional assets like stocks and bonds.
- **Innovation and Growth**: Investing in cryptocurrencies allows investors to participate in the growth of innovative technologies and applications. Blockchain technology is transforming various industries, from finance to supply chain management, creating numerous investment opportunities.
- **Liquidity**: Many cryptocurrencies are highly liquid, with large trading volumes on various exchanges. This liquidity allows investors to enter and exit positions with relative ease compared to other asset classes.

- **Access and Inclusion**: Cryptocurrencies provide financial access and inclusion for people who are underserved by traditional financial systems. This democratization of finance can lead to increased adoption and value appreciation.

Risks of Cryptocurrency Investment

- **Volatility**: Cryptocurrencies are known for their extreme price volatility. Significant price swings can occur within short periods, leading to substantial gains or losses. Investors must be prepared for this volatility and manage their risk accordingly.
- **Regulatory Uncertainty**: The regulatory environment for cryptocurrencies is still evolving and varies significantly across different jurisdictions. Regulatory changes can impact the value and legality of certain cryptocurrencies, posing risks to investors.
- **Security Risks**: While blockchain technology is inherently secure, the broader ecosystem is not immune to hacking, fraud, and theft. Exchange hacks, phishing attacks, and smart contract vulnerabilities are common threats that can result in the loss of funds.
- **Market Manipulation**: The relatively unregulated nature of cryptocurrency markets makes them susceptible to manipulation. Pump-and-dump schemes, insider trading, and market manipulation by large holders (whales) can distort prices and impact investments.
- **Lack of Fundamental Analysis**: Unlike traditional assets, cryptocurrencies often lack the fundamental analysis metrics that investors rely on. This can make it challenging to assess the intrinsic value of a cryptocurrency and make informed investment decisions.

- **Technological Risks**: Blockchain and cryptocurrency projects depend on the underlying technology. Bugs, technical failures, or vulnerabilities in the blockchain can have severe implications for the value and functionality of a cryptocurrency.

Strategies for Managing Risks

- **Research and Due Diligence**: Conduct thorough research on any cryptocurrency or blockchain project before investing. Understand the technology, use case, team, market potential, and competitive landscape.
- **Diversification**: Spread your investment across multiple cryptocurrencies and other asset classes to mitigate risk. Diversification can help reduce the impact of a poor-performing asset on your overall portfolio.
- **Risk Management**: Use risk management techniques such as setting stop-loss orders, position sizing, and portfolio rebalancing. Only invest what you can afford to lose and avoid leveraging or margin trading unless you are an experienced trader.
- **Secure Storage**: Store your cryptocurrencies in secure wallets, preferably hardware wallets, to protect against hacking and theft. Avoid keeping large amounts of funds on exchanges.
- **Stay Informed**: Keep up to date with the latest developments in the cryptocurrency space, including regulatory changes, technological advancements, and market trends. Staying informed will help you make timely and informed decisions.

Investing in cryptocurrencies and blockchain technology can be highly rewarding, offering the potential for significant returns and participation in groundbreaking innovations. However, the market is fraught with risks, including volatility, regulatory uncertainty, security threats, and market manipulation. By understanding these risks and implementing effective risk management strategies, investors can navigate the cryptocurrency landscape more confidently and make informed decisions that align with their investment goals. As with any investment, a balanced approach, thorough research, and a clear understanding of your risk tolerance are essential for success in the world of digital assets.

5.5. Long-Term Investment Strategies

Long-term investment strategies in cryptocurrencies and blockchain technology focus on the potential for significant returns over an extended period. These strategies require patience, thorough research, and a disciplined approach to managing risks and rewards. In this section, we'll explore effective long-term investment strategies to help you build a resilient and profitable portfolio in the evolving landscape of digital assets.

1. HODLing

- **Definition**: "HODL" is a term derived from a misspelling of "hold" and stands for "Hold On for Dear Life." It represents a long-term investment strategy where investors buy and hold onto cryptocurrencies, regardless of market volatility, with the expectation that their value will increase over time.

- **Benefits:**

  - o Minimizes the impact of short-term market fluctuations.
  - o Reduces transaction fees and capital gains taxes associated with frequent trading.
  - o Capitalizes on the long-term growth potential of high-quality cryptocurrencies.

- **Implementation**: Choose a diversified portfolio of established cryptocurrencies with strong fundamentals, such as Bitcoin and Ethereum. Hold these assets in secure wallets and avoid the temptation to sell during market downturns.

2. Dollar-cost averaging (DCA)

- **Definition**: Dollar-cost averaging is an investment strategy where you invest a fixed amount of money at regular intervals, regardless of the cryptocurrency's price. This approach helps mitigate the impact of market volatility by spreading your investment over time.

- **Benefits**:

  - o Reduces the risk of investing a large sum during market peaks.
  - o Smooth out the effects of price volatility by averaging purchase prices over time.

o Encourages disciplined investing and removes emotional decision-making.

- **Implementation**: Set a regular investment schedule (e.g., weekly, monthly) and invest a consistent amount in your chosen cryptocurrencies. Automate the process if possible, using features offered by some exchanges and investment platforms.

3. Research and Due Diligence

- **Fundamental Analysis**: Conduct thorough research on each cryptocurrency or blockchain project before investing. Analyze the technology, use case, team, market potential, and competitive landscape.
- **Whitepapers and Roadmaps**: Review the project's whitepaper and development roadmap to understand its goals, milestones, and progress. Look for transparency and a clear vision for the future.
- **Community and Adoption**: Evaluate the strength and activity of the project's community. A strong, engaged community can be a positive indicator of a project's potential for long-term success. Also, consider the level of adoption and partnerships with established companies or organizations.

4. Diversification

- **Portfolio Diversification**: Spread your investments across a variety of cryptocurrencies and blockchain projects to reduce risk. Include a mix of large-cap cryptocurrencies like Bitcoin and Ethereum, as well as promising altcoins with growth potential.

- **Asset Class Diversification**: Consider diversifying into other asset classes, such as stocks, bonds, real estate, and precious metals, to further reduce risk and create a balanced investment portfolio.

5. Staying Informed and Adapting

- **Continuous Learning**: Stay up to date with the latest developments in the cryptocurrency and blockchain space. Follow reputable news sources, join online communities, and participate in industry events to stay informed.
- **Regulatory Awareness**: Keep track of regulatory changes and their potential impact on your investments. Regulatory developments can significantly influence the value and legality of cryptocurrencies.
- **Adaptability**: Be prepared to adjust your investment strategy as the market evolves. This may involve reallocating assets, exiting underperforming investments, or adding new promising projects to your portfolio.

6. Security Practices

- **Secure Storage**: Use hardware wallets or other secure storage solutions to protect your cryptocurrencies from hacking and theft. Avoid keeping large amounts of funds on exchanges.

- **Private Keys and Backups**: Safeguard your private keys and create backups of your wallet's recovery phrases. Store these in a secure, offline location.
- **Two-Factor Authentication (2FA)**: Enable 2FA on your exchange and wallet accounts to add an extra layer of security.

Long-term investment strategies in cryptocurrencies and blockchain technology require a disciplined approach, thorough research, and a focus on security. By adopting strategies such as HODLing, dollar-cost averaging, diversification, and staying informed, investors can navigate the volatile cryptocurrency market and capitalize on its long-term growth potential. Building a resilient and profitable portfolio in the digital asset space involves balancing risk and reward, continually adapting to new developments, and maintaining a long-term perspective. As the cryptocurrency ecosystem continues to evolve, these strategies will help investors achieve their financial goals and participate in the transformative potential of blockchain technology.

Chapter 6: The Regulatory Landscape and Legal Considerations

The evolution of industries, especially those driven by rapid technological advancements, often outpaces the regulatory frameworks designed to govern them. Navigating the intricate web of regulations and legal considerations is akin to walking a tightrope – a delicate balance between innovation and compliance. This chapter delves into the regulatory landscape and legal intricacies that organizations must traverse to ensure lawful and ethical operations.

The Foundations of Regulatory Frameworks

Regulatory frameworks are the bedrock of orderly and lawful conduct in any industry. They are designed to protect consumers, ensure fair competition, and maintain market integrity. These frameworks vary significantly across regions and sectors, shaped by historical precedents, economic imperatives, and societal values.

Historical Context

Understanding the historical context of regulations offers insight into their current structure and function. For instance, the financial sector's regulatory environment in the United States is largely a product of the Great Depression. The collapse of the stock market in 1929 led to the establishment of the Securities and Exchange Commission (SEC) in 1934 to restore investor confidence and stabilize financial markets.

Similarly, the rise of the digital age has seen the introduction of regulations like the General Data Protection Regulation (GDPR) in the European Union. Enacted in 2018, GDPR was a response to growing concerns over data privacy and the power of tech giants. It represents a significant shift in how personal data is handled, imposing stringent requirements on organizations worldwide.

Regional Variations

While some regulations have global reach, many are region-specific. The differences can be stark, affecting how multinational companies operate. For instance, environmental regulations in the European Union tend to be more stringent than in other parts of the world. The EU's Emissions Trading System (ETS), established in 2005, is a cornerstone of its climate policy, mandating carbon allowances for companies and fostering a market for trading these permits.

In contrast, the United States has historically taken a more decentralized approach to environmental regulation. The Clean Air Act of 1970 and the Clean Water Act of 1972 laid the groundwork, but enforcement and specific standards can vary widely between states. Companies operating in multiple jurisdictions must navigate these variations to maintain compliance.

Legal Considerations in the Digital Age

The digital revolution has introduced unprecedented challenges and opportunities. As businesses increasingly operate online, issues such as data privacy, cybersecurity, and intellectual property have come to the forefront.

Data Privacy and Protection

Data is often touted as the new oil, but its extraction, storage, and use come with significant responsibilities. The GDPR has set a high bar for data protection, requiring explicit consent from individuals for data processing and granting them rights to access, correct, and delete their data. Non-compliance can result in hefty fines, as seen in the cases against tech giants like Google and Facebook.

The United States has yet to implement a federal data protection law akin to the GDPR. Instead, it relies on a patchwork of state laws and sector-specific regulations, such as the California Consumer Privacy Act (CCPA), which grants Californians similar rights over their data. Companies must stay abreast of these evolving laws to avoid legal pitfalls.

Cybersecurity Regulations

As cyber threats become more sophisticated, regulatory bodies have stepped up their efforts to safeguard critical infrastructure and sensitive information. The introduction of the Cybersecurity Information Sharing Act (CISA) in the U.S. in 2015 encourages private companies to share information about cyber threats with the government to enhance collective security.

In the financial sector, regulations like the New York Department of Financial Services (NYDFS) Cybersecurity Regulation require financial institutions to implement robust cybersecurity programs, conduct regular risk assessments, and report cybersecurity events. These measures aim to protect both the financial system and consumers from the fallout of cyber attacks.

Intellectual Property in the Digital Era

The digital age has also transformed the landscape of intellectual property (IP). The ease of copying and distributing digital content poses significant challenges for IP protection. Regulations such as the Digital Millennium Copyright Act (DMCA) in the U.S. aim to protect copyright holders while also addressing the realities of the internet, such as safe harbor provisions for online platforms that host user-generated content.

Moreover, the rise of artificial intelligence and machine learning introduces new complexities. Questions around the ownership of AI-generated works and the use of copyrighted material for training algorithms are at the forefront of legal debates. The resolution of these issues will shape the future of innovation and creativity in the digital age.

Compliance Strategies for Modern Businesses

Navigating the regulatory landscape requires a proactive and strategic approach. Companies must develop robust compliance programs that not only adhere to current regulations but also anticipate future changes.

Building a Compliance Framework

A strong compliance framework starts with a thorough understanding of applicable regulations. This involves conducting regular audits, staying informed about legislative developments, and engaging with legal experts. Companies should also foster a culture of compliance, where employees at all levels are aware of and committed to regulatory requirements.

Leveraging Technology

Technology can be a powerful ally in ensuring compliance. Regulatory technology, or RegTech, encompasses a range of solutions designed to streamline compliance processes. From automated monitoring systems that flag potential issues to data analytics tools that provide insights into regulatory risks, RegTech can enhance a company's ability to stay compliant.

Continuous Education and Training

Regulations are not static; they evolve in response to new challenges and societal shifts. Continuous education and training are essential to keep pace with these changes. Companies should invest in regular training programs for their employees, ensuring that they are up-to-date with the latest regulatory requirements and best practices.

The Future of Regulation

As industries continue to evolve, so too will the regulatory landscape. Emerging technologies like blockchain, artificial intelligence, and quantum computing present both opportunities and challenges for regulators. Striking the right balance between fostering innovation and protecting the public will be key.

Adaptive Regulation

One promising approach is adaptive regulation, which involves creating flexible regulatory frameworks that can evolve alongside technological advancements. This can be seen in the regulatory sandboxes established by financial regulators in the UK and Singapore, where companies can test innovative products and services in a controlled environment before they are fully launched.

Global Harmonization

In an increasingly interconnected world, there is also a push towards global harmonization of regulations. Organizations like the International Organization for Standardization (ISO) and the Financial Stability Board (FSB) work towards creating common standards that facilitate international trade and cooperation. While complete harmonization may be elusive, these efforts can reduce regulatory fragmentation and create a more predictable operating environment for businesses.

Ethical Considerations

Finally, ethical considerations are becoming an integral part of the regulatory dialogue. Issues such as algorithmic bias, data privacy, and the environmental impact of technology are prompting regulators to consider not just the legal, but also the ethical implications of technological advancements. Companies that prioritize ethical practices will be better positioned to navigate the regulatory landscape and build trust with their stakeholders.

In conclusion, the regulatory landscape is a complex and dynamic domain that requires constant vigilance and adaptability. By understanding the historical context, staying informed about current and emerging regulations, and adopting proactive compliance strategies, companies can navigate this landscape successfully. As we look to the future, the interplay between regulation, innovation, and ethics will shape the path forward, creating both challenges and opportunities for businesses and society at large.

6.1. Global Regulatory Perspectives on Blockchain and Cryptocurrency

Blockchain technology and cryptocurrencies have emerged as transformative forces in the digital age, promising to revolutionize various sectors from finance to supply chain management. However, their disruptive potential also poses significant regulatory challenges. Governments and regulatory bodies worldwide are grappling with how to harness the benefits of these technologies while mitigating risks such as fraud, money laundering, and market instability. This section explores the diverse regulatory approaches taken by different countries and regions, highlighting the evolving global landscape of blockchain and cryptocurrency regulation.

The United States: A Fragmented Approach

In the United States, the regulatory environment for blockchain and cryptocurrencies is characterized by a patchwork of federal and state-level regulations. Various agencies, including the Securities and Exchange Commission (SEC), the Commodity Futures Trading

Commission (CFTC), and the Financial Crimes Enforcement Network (FinCEN), play crucial roles in this fragmented landscape.

The SEC primarily focuses on whether cryptocurrencies and initial coin offerings (ICOs) constitute securities. If deemed securities, they are subject to stringent regulatory requirements under U.S. securities laws. For instance, the SEC's lawsuit against Ripple Labs in 2020, alleging that its XRP token was an unregistered security, underscored the agency's commitment to enforcing compliance in the crypto space.

Meanwhile, the CFTC views certain cryptocurrencies as commodities and regulates their trading under the Commodity Exchange Act. In addition, FinCEN requires cryptocurrency exchanges and wallet providers to comply with anti-money laundering (AML) and know-your-customer (KYC) regulations, aimed at preventing illicit activities.

Individual states also impose their regulations, further complicating the landscape. New York's BitLicense, introduced in 2015, is one of the most stringent state-level frameworks, requiring companies dealing with virtual currencies to obtain a special license and adhere to rigorous standards.

The European Union: Striving for Harmonization

The European Union has taken significant steps toward creating a unified regulatory framework for blockchain and cryptocurrencies. The Markets in Crypto-Assets (MiCA) regulation, proposed in 2020, aims to provide legal certainty and protect consumers and investors across the EU. MiCA seeks to establish a comprehensive set of rules for crypto-assets not covered by existing financial services legislation.

MiCA addresses various aspects, including the issuance of crypto-assets, the operation of trading platforms, and the responsibilities of crypto-asset service providers. It also introduces stringent requirements for stablecoins, which are digital currencies pegged to traditional assets like the euro or the U.S. dollar, to ensure financial stability.

Moreover, the EU's Fifth Anti-Money Laundering Directive (5AMLD), implemented in 2020, extended AML and KYC obligations to cryptocurrency exchanges and wallet providers. This directive mandates that these entities register with national authorities and comply with AML regulations, enhancing the transparency and security of crypto transactions within the EU.

China: A Strict Stance

China has adopted one of the most restrictive regulatory approaches toward cryptocurrencies. The Chinese government has banned cryptocurrency exchanges and initial coin offerings, citing concerns over financial stability and the potential for illicit activities. In 2021, China intensified its crackdown by declaring all cryptocurrency transactions illegal and banning cryptocurrency mining, which had previously flourished in regions with abundant energy resources.

Despite its stringent stance on cryptocurrencies, China has shown keen interest in blockchain technology. The government actively supports the development of blockchain applications in various sectors and has launched the Digital Currency Electronic Payment (DCEP) system, a state-backed digital currency also known as the digital yuan. This dual approach reflects China's strategy to harness the benefits of blockchain technology while maintaining strict control over the financial system.

Japan: A Progressive Regulatory Environment

Japan is often regarded as one of the most crypto-friendly countries, with a progressive regulatory environment that aims to balance innovation and consumer protection. The Payment Services Act (PSA) and the Financial Instruments and Exchange Act (FIEA) provide the legal framework for cryptocurrency exchanges and token offerings in Japan.

Under the PSA, cryptocurrency exchanges must register with the Financial Services Agency (FSA) and comply with AML and KYC regulations. The FIEA, amended in 2020, introduced stricter rules for security token offerings (STOs), treating them similarly to traditional securities to protect investors.

Japan's regulatory clarity and proactive approach have made it an attractive hub for blockchain and cryptocurrency businesses. The country's support for innovation is further evidenced by initiatives like the regulatory sandbox, which allows companies to test new products and services under a controlled environment with regulatory oversight.

Emerging Markets: Varied Approaches

Emerging markets are also shaping their regulatory landscapes in response to the rise of blockchain and cryptocurrencies. Countries like India, Brazil, and Nigeria are exploring ways to regulate the sector while fostering innovation.

India's regulatory stance has been evolving, with the government initially proposing a blanket ban on cryptocurrencies but later considering a more balanced approach. The proposed Cryptocurrency and Regulation of Official Digital Currency Bill aims to prohibit private cryptocurrencies while supporting the development of a central bank digital currency (CBDC).

Brazil has taken steps to regulate the crypto industry through legislation that defines cryptocurrencies and establishes guidelines for their use. The Central Bank of Brazil is also exploring the development of a CBDC, reflecting a broader trend among central banks worldwide.

In Nigeria, the Central Bank issued a directive in 2021 prohibiting financial institutions from facilitating cryptocurrency transactions, citing concerns over financial stability and the potential for illicit activities. However, the country remains a significant market for cryptocurrencies, driven by factors such as economic instability and the need for financial inclusion.

The Future of Blockchain and Cryptocurrency Regulation

The regulatory landscape for blockchain and cryptocurrencies is continually evolving, influenced by technological advancements, market dynamics, and societal needs. As these technologies mature, regulatory frameworks are likely to become more sophisticated, aiming to strike a balance between fostering innovation and ensuring consumer protection and financial stability.

Global cooperation and harmonization of regulations will be crucial in addressing the cross-border nature of blockchain and cryptocurrencies. Organizations like the Financial Action Task Force (FATF) play a pivotal role in setting international standards for AML and combating the financing of terrorism (CFT), providing guidelines that influence national regulations.

Moreover, the integration of ethical considerations into regulatory frameworks will be essential as blockchain technology intersects with issues such as data privacy, environmental impact, and social equity. By adopting a holistic approach to regulation, governments, and regulatory bodies can support the sustainable growth of the blockchain and cryptocurrency sectors, unlocking their full potential for innovation and societal benefit.

6.2. Legal Challenges and Compliance Issues

The rise of blockchain and cryptocurrency technologies has not only revolutionized various industries but has also introduced a host of legal challenges and compliance issues. As businesses and individuals increasingly adopt these technologies, they must navigate a complex and evolving legal landscape. This section examines the key legal challenges and compliance issues associated with blockchain and cryptocurrencies, highlighting the need for robust legal strategies and regulatory compliance frameworks.

Legal Challenges in Blockchain and Cryptocurrencies

1. Regulatory Uncertainty

One of the primary legal challenges facing blockchain and cryptocurrency companies is regulatory uncertainty. The rapid pace of technological innovation often outstrips the ability of regulators to create clear and comprehensive legal frameworks. This uncertainty can deter investment, stifle innovation, and create compliance risks for businesses.

For example, the classification of cryptocurrencies varies significantly across jurisdictions. In some countries, cryptocurrencies are considered securities, while in others, they are treated as commodities, property, or even legal tender. This lack of uniformity makes it challenging for companies operating in multiple regions to develop consistent compliance strategies.

2. Security and Privacy Concerns

Blockchain technology, while inherently secure due to its decentralized and immutable nature, still faces significant security and privacy challenges. Smart contracts, which are self-executing contracts with the terms directly written into code, can be vulnerable to bugs and exploits. High-profile hacks and breaches, such as the DAO attack in 2016, have highlighted these vulnerabilities and the need for rigorous security measures.

Privacy concerns also arise, particularly with public blockchains where transaction data is visible to all participants. While pseudonymous, blockchain transactions can sometimes be traced back to individuals, raising issues of data privacy and protection. Compliance with data protection laws like the European Union's General Data Protection Regulation (GDPR) can be challenging, given the immutable nature of blockchain records.

3. Intellectual Property Rights

Intellectual property (IP) rights in the context of blockchain and cryptocurrencies present another complex legal challenge. The decentralized nature of blockchain makes it difficult to determine ownership and enforce IP rights. For instance, the creation of non-fungible tokens (NFTs) has raised questions about copyright infringement and the authenticity of digital assets.

Additionally, the use of existing copyrighted material in blockchain projects, such as in the training of AI algorithms or the creation of digital content, can lead to IP disputes. Determining the rightful owner and enforcing IP rights in a decentralized ecosystem requires innovative legal solutions and international cooperation.

Compliance Issues in Blockchain and Cryptocurrencies

1. **Anti-Money Laundering (AML) and Counter-Terrorism Financing (CTF)**

AML and CTF regulations are critical components of the compliance landscape for blockchain and cryptocurrency companies. Due to the pseudonymous nature of cryptocurrency transactions, they are often perceived as a potential tool for money laundering and terrorist financing. Regulatory bodies worldwide have introduced stringent AML and CTF requirements to mitigate these risks.

Compliance with these regulations typically involves implementing robust KYC procedures to verify the identities of customers, monitoring transactions for suspicious activity, and reporting any suspicious transactions to relevant authorities. However, the decentralized nature of many blockchain platforms can complicate these compliance efforts.

2. Tax Compliance

Tax compliance is another significant issue for individuals and businesses dealing with cryptocurrencies. Tax authorities in various countries have begun to issue guidance on the taxation of cryptocurrency transactions, but the rules can vary widely. For example, in the United States, the Internal Revenue Service (IRS) treats cryptocurrencies as property, subjecting transactions to capital gains tax.

Cryptocurrency users must keep detailed records of their transactions to accurately report gains and losses. The anonymous nature of cryptocurrencies can also pose challenges for tax authorities in tracking and enforcing compliance, leading to calls for greater transparency and reporting requirements.

3. Consumer Protection

Consumer protection is a critical aspect of regulatory compliance for blockchain and cryptocurrency businesses. Given the high volatility of cryptocurrency markets and the prevalence of scams and fraudulent schemes, regulators aim to protect consumers from undue risks.

Compliance measures may include providing clear and transparent information about the risks associated with cryptocurrency investments, implementing measures to prevent fraud and market manipulation, and ensuring that consumers have recourse in the event of disputes or losses. Regulatory frameworks like the EU's MiCA are designed to enhance consumer protection in the crypto space.

4. Licensing and Operational Requirements

Many jurisdictions require cryptocurrency businesses to obtain specific licenses to operate legally. These licenses may include requirements for minimum capital reserves, cybersecurity measures, and operational transparency. For example, in New York, the BitLicense framework imposes rigorous licensing requirements on cryptocurrency businesses.

Meeting these licensing and operational requirements can be resource-intensive, particularly for startups and smaller businesses. However, obtaining the necessary licenses is crucial for legal compliance and building trust with consumers and investors.

Developing Effective Compliance Strategies

Navigating the legal challenges and compliance issues in the blockchain and cryptocurrency space requires a proactive and strategic approach. Businesses must develop comprehensive compliance programs that address regulatory requirements and mitigate legal risks.

1. Staying Informed and Engaged

Keeping abreast of regulatory developments and engaging with regulators is essential for compliance. Businesses should monitor legislative changes, participate in industry forums, and engage in dialogue with regulators to understand evolving requirements and advocate for favorable regulatory environments.

2. Implementing Robust Compliance Programs

Developing and implementing robust compliance programs is critical. This includes establishing internal policies and procedures for AML and CTF compliance, data protection, and consumer protection. Regular audits and risk assessments can help identify potential compliance gaps and areas for improvement.

3. Leveraging Technology for Compliance

Regulatory technology (RegTech) solutions can enhance compliance efforts by automating and streamlining processes. These solutions can include tools for KYC verification, transaction monitoring, and regulatory reporting. Leveraging blockchain's inherent transparency and immutability can also support compliance by providing auditable records of transactions.

4. Legal Expertise and Training

Engaging legal experts with specialized knowledge of blockchain and cryptocurrency law is crucial for navigating the complex legal landscape. Regular training for employees on regulatory requirements and compliance best practices can also help ensure that businesses remain compliant and can respond effectively to regulatory changes.

In conclusion, while the legal challenges and compliance issues associated with blockchain and cryptocurrencies are significant, they are not insurmountable. By understanding the regulatory landscape, implementing effective compliance strategies, and staying informed about legal developments, businesses can navigate these challenges successfully and harness the transformative potential of blockchain and cryptocurrencies.

6.3. The Role of Governments and Central Banks

Governments and central banks play pivotal roles in shaping the regulatory and economic environment for blockchain and cryptocurrencies. Their actions can significantly influence the adoption, integration, and stability of these technologies within the global financial system. This section explores the diverse roles that governments and central banks assume in the context of blockchain and cryptocurrencies, highlighting their impact on regulation, innovation, and economic stability.

Governments: Policy Makers and Regulators

1. Creating Regulatory Frameworks

Governments are responsible for establishing the regulatory frameworks that govern blockchain and cryptocurrency activities. These frameworks aim to balance innovation with consumer protection, financial stability, and the prevention of illicit activities. The approaches taken by different governments can vary widely, reflecting their unique economic conditions, legal traditions, and policy priorities.

For instance, the European Union's Markets in Crypto-Assets (MiCA) regulation seeks to create a unified legal framework for cryptocurrencies across member states, providing clarity and protection for consumers while fostering innovation. In contrast, China has implemented strict regulations, including bans on cryptocurrency trading and mining, to maintain financial control and stability.

2. Taxation Policies

Taxation policies are another critical area where governments exert influence. By defining how cryptocurrencies are taxed, governments can shape the behavior of individuals and businesses. In the United States, the Internal Revenue Service (IRS) treats cryptocurrencies as property, subjecting transactions to capital gains tax. Other countries, like Germany, offer more favorable tax treatments for long-term cryptocurrency holdings, encouraging investment.

Clear and consistent tax policies are essential for ensuring compliance and fostering a predictable business environment. Ambiguous or overly burdensome tax regulations can hinder the growth of the cryptocurrency sector and drive activities underground.

3. Anti-Money Laundering (AML) and Counter-Terrorism Financing (CTF)

Governments play a crucial role in implementing AML and CTF measures to prevent the misuse of cryptocurrencies for illicit purposes. This includes setting requirements for cryptocurrency exchanges and service providers to implement KYC procedures, monitor transactions, and report suspicious activities.

International cooperation is vital in this area, as illicit activities often transcend national borders. Organizations like the Financial Action Task

Force (FATF) provide global standards and guidelines for AML and CTF compliance, influencing national regulations and fostering international collaboration.

Central Banks: Guardians of Financial Stability

1. Central Bank Digital Currencies (CBDCs)

One of the most significant developments involving central banks and blockchain technology is the exploration and implementation of central bank digital currencies (CBDCs). CBDCs represent digital forms of a country's fiat currency, issued and regulated by the central bank. They aim to enhance payment systems, increase financial inclusion, and provide a secure and efficient means of transaction.

Countries like China, with its Digital Currency Electronic Payment (DCEP) system, are at the forefront of CBDC development. The digital yuan aims to complement the existing financial system, reduce reliance on cash, and enhance the central bank's control over the monetary supply.

In contrast, the European Central Bank (ECB) is in the research and experimentation phase with its proposed digital euro, exploring potential benefits and challenges. The ECB aims to ensure that a digital euro would be resilient, and secure, and provide a level of privacy for users while preventing illicit activities.

2. Monetary Policy and Financial Stability

Central banks are also responsible for maintaining monetary policy and financial stability. The rise of cryptocurrencies presents both opportunities and challenges in this regard. On the one hand, cryptocurrencies can provide new tools for monetary policy, such as programmable money with conditions attached to its use. On the other hand, the volatility and speculative nature of many cryptocurrencies can pose risks to financial stability.

Central banks must carefully monitor the impact of cryptocurrencies on traditional financial systems and consider regulatory measures to mitigate risks. This includes setting guidelines for financial institutions' exposure to cryptocurrencies and developing frameworks for integrating digital assets into the broader financial ecosystem.

3. Promoting Innovation and Research

Central banks can play a proactive role in promoting innovation and research in blockchain technology. By supporting pilot projects, research initiatives, and regulatory sandboxes, central banks can foster a better understanding of blockchain's potential and its implications for the financial system.

For example, the Bank of England has engaged in various research projects to explore the potential of distributed ledger technology (DLT) in areas such as cross-border payments and settlement systems. By encouraging experimentation and collaboration with private sector innovators, central banks can help shape the future of financial technology.

International Collaboration and Standardization

Given the global nature of blockchain and cryptocurrencies, international collaboration and standardization are essential. Governments and central banks must work together to create coherent regulatory frameworks that minimize arbitrage opportunities and ensure consistent protections across borders.

Organizations like the International Monetary Fund (IMF), the World Bank, and the Bank for International Settlements (BIS) play crucial roles in facilitating dialogue and cooperation among nations. These organizations help develop international standards, provide technical assistance, and promote best practices in regulating and integrating blockchain technologies.

Balancing Innovation and Regulation

The challenge for governments and central banks lies in balancing the need to foster innovation with the imperative to protect consumers and ensure financial stability. Overly restrictive regulations can stifle innovation and drive activities to less regulated jurisdictions, while insufficient regulation can lead to market instability and abuse.

Achieving this balance requires a nuanced and adaptive regulatory approach. Governments and central banks must stay informed about technological advancements, engage with industry stakeholders, and be willing to adjust regulations as the market evolves. By adopting a collaborative and flexible approach, they can support the sustainable growth of blockchain and cryptocurrencies, unlocking their potential benefits for the economy and society.

In conclusion, the roles of governments and central banks are crucial in shaping the future of blockchain and cryptocurrencies. Through effective regulation, proactive innovation, and international collaboration, they can help navigate the challenges and opportunities presented by these transformative technologies, ensuring their integration into the global financial system is secure, inclusive, and beneficial for all.

6.4. Tax Implications of Cryptocurrency Transactions

Cryptocurrency transactions have significant tax implications that individuals and businesses must understand and comply with. While cryptocurrencies offer certain advantages, such as decentralized transactions and privacy, they also present unique challenges for tax authorities due to their digital and cross-border nature. This section examines the tax considerations associated with various cryptocurrency transactions, including buying, selling, trading, and mining, highlighting key principles and best practices for tax compliance.

Classification of Cryptocurrencies for Tax Purposes

1. Property vs. Currency

The classification of cryptocurrencies for tax purposes varies by jurisdiction. In many countries, including the United States, cryptocurrencies are treated as property rather than currency. This means that cryptocurrency transactions are subject to capital gains tax, similar to transactions involving stocks or real estate.

As property, each cryptocurrency transaction triggers a taxable event, with gains or losses calculated based on the difference between the purchase price and the selling price. Short-term capital gains, from assets held for less than a year, are taxed at ordinary income tax rates, while long-term capital gains, from assets held for over a year, are taxed at lower rates.

2. Currency vs. Commodity

In some jurisdictions, cryptocurrencies are treated as currency or commodities rather than property. This can have significant taxation implications, as currency transactions may be subject to different tax rates or exemptions.

For example, in Japan, cryptocurrencies are classified as legal tender, subjecting transactions to consumption tax but exempting them from capital gains tax. In Australia, cryptocurrencies are treated as property for individuals and as commodities for businesses, with different tax treatments based on the nature of the transaction.

Tax Considerations for Cryptocurrency Transactions

1. Buying and Selling

The purchase and sale of cryptocurrencies are taxable events, with gains or losses realized upon disposal. When calculating taxable gains, individuals must account for transaction fees, exchange rates, and any other associated costs.

For example, if an individual purchases one bitcoin for $10,000 and later sells it for $15,000, they would realize a taxable gain of $5,000. This gain would be subject to capital gains tax, based on the holding period of the asset.

2. Trading

Cryptocurrency trading, involving the frequent buying and selling of assets for short-term gains, can result in complex tax implications. Each trade is considered a taxable event, requiring individuals to track the cost basis and fair market value of each asset at the time of acquisition and disposal.

Traders may also be subject to additional reporting requirements, such as filing Form 8949 and Schedule D with their tax returns in the United States. Failure to accurately report trading activity can result in penalties and fines from tax authorities.

3. Mining

Cryptocurrency mining, the process of validating transactions and adding them to the blockchain, can generate taxable income. Miners receive newly created coins as rewards for their efforts, which are considered taxable income at the fair market value on the date of receipt.

In addition to mining rewards, miners may also incur expenses related to equipment, electricity, and maintenance, which can be deducted as business expenses. Proper record-keeping and documentation are essential for calculating taxable income accurately.

Tax Reporting and Compliance

1. Record-Keeping

Accurate record-keeping is essential for cryptocurrency tax reporting and compliance. Individuals and businesses should maintain detailed records of all cryptocurrency transactions, including dates, transaction amounts, cost basis, fair market value, and any associated expenses.

Various software tools and platforms are available to help automate and streamline record-keeping processes, making it easier to track and report cryptocurrency transactions for tax purposes.

2. Reporting Requirements

Tax authorities worldwide are increasingly focused on cryptocurrency tax compliance, issuing guidance and enforcement measures to ensure taxpayers accurately report their crypto-related income and gains.

In the United States, for example, the IRS has made cryptocurrency tax compliance a priority, sending warning letters and audits to individuals suspected of underreporting or failing to report cryptocurrency transactions. The IRS has also updated tax forms and instructions to include specific questions about cryptocurrency transactions.

Seeking Professional Advice

Given the complexity and evolving nature of cryptocurrency taxation, individuals and businesses are encouraged to seek professional advice from tax advisors and accountants with expertise in cryptocurrency taxation.

Tax professionals can provide personalized guidance on tax planning strategies, compliance requirements, and reporting obligations based on individual circumstances and jurisdictional requirements.

In conclusion, the tax implications of cryptocurrency transactions are multifaceted and require careful consideration and compliance. Individuals and businesses must understand the classification of cryptocurrencies for tax purposes, track all transactions accurately, and adhere to reporting and compliance requirements to avoid penalties and fines from tax authorities.

By maintaining detailed records, seeking professional advice, and staying informed about regulatory developments, taxpayers can navigate the complex landscape of cryptocurrency taxation effectively and ensure compliance with tax laws and regulations.

6.5. Future Directions in Regulation

The regulation of blockchain and cryptocurrencies is a dynamic and evolving field, shaped by technological advancements, market dynamics, and societal needs. As these technologies continue to mature and gain mainstream acceptance, regulators face the challenge of balancing innovation with consumer protection, financial stability, and regulatory compliance. This section explores future directions in regulation for blockchain and cryptocurrencies, highlighting key trends, challenges, and opportunities on the horizon.

1. Enhanced Regulatory Clarity

One of the most pressing needs in the regulation of blockchain and cryptocurrencies is enhanced regulatory clarity. Many jurisdictions lack clear and comprehensive regulatory frameworks for these technologies, leading to uncertainty and inconsistency in how they are treated.

In the coming years, we can expect regulators to focus on providing clearer guidance and standards for blockchain and cryptocurrency activities. This may involve updating existing regulations, issuing new guidelines, and engaging with industry stakeholders to develop coherent and practical regulatory frameworks.

2. Global Harmonization

Given the global nature of blockchain and cryptocurrencies, there is a growing recognition of the need for international cooperation and harmonization of regulations. Fragmented regulatory approaches across different jurisdictions can create regulatory arbitrage opportunities, hinder innovation, and pose challenges for cross-border transactions.

In the future, we are likely to see increased efforts towards global harmonization of regulations, with organizations like the Financial Stability Board (FSB), the International Organization of Securities Commissions (IOSCO), and the Financial Action Task Force (FATF) playing key roles in setting international standards and best practices.

3. Focus on Consumer Protection

Consumer protection will remain a top priority for regulators as blockchain and cryptocurrencies become more integrated into mainstream finance. The decentralized and pseudonymous nature of these technologies can expose consumers to risks such as fraud, hacking, and market manipulation.

Regulators will seek to enhance consumer protection measures by imposing requirements for transparency, disclosure, and investor education. This may include mandating clear disclosures about the risks associated with cryptocurrency investments, implementing measures to prevent fraud and scams, and ensuring that consumers have recourse in the event of disputes or losses.

4. Embracing Innovation

While regulators must address risks and protect consumers, they also recognize the potential of blockchain and cryptocurrencies to drive innovation and economic growth. In the future, we can expect regulators to adopt a more nuanced and adaptive approach that fosters innovation while ensuring regulatory compliance.

This may involve creating regulatory sandboxes and innovation hubs where companies can test new products and services in a controlled environment with regulatory oversight. Regulators may also explore regulatory frameworks that are more conducive to innovation, such as flexible licensing regimes and streamlined approval processes.

5. Addressing Emerging Challenges

As blockchain and cryptocurrencies continue to evolve, regulators will need to adapt to emerging challenges and risks. These may include issues such as the rise of decentralized finance (DeFi), the proliferation of stablecoins, and the integration of blockchain into supply chain management and other industries.

Regulators will need to stay abreast of these developments and proactively address potential risks and concerns. This may involve conducting research, engaging with industry stakeholders, and developing targeted regulations and enforcement mechanisms to address emerging challenges effectively.

6. Ethical and Social Considerations

In addition to economic and technical considerations, regulators are increasingly focused on the ethical and social implications of blockchain and cryptocurrencies. Issues such as data privacy, algorithmic bias, environmental sustainability, and social equity are becoming integral parts of the regulatory dialogue.

In the future, we can expect regulators to incorporate ethical considerations into their decision-making processes and regulatory frameworks. This may involve conducting impact assessments to evaluate the potential social and environmental consequences of new regulations, engaging with stakeholders from diverse backgrounds, and promoting inclusive and responsible innovation in the blockchain and cryptocurrency space.

The future of regulation for blockchain and cryptocurrencies will be shaped by a combination of technological advancements, market dynamics, and regulatory responses. By embracing innovation, enhancing consumer protection, fostering global cooperation, and addressing emerging challenges, regulators can create a more resilient, inclusive, and sustainable regulatory environment that supports the continued growth and development of blockchain and cryptocurrencies for the benefit of society as a whole.

Chapter 7: How You Can Benefit from Blockchain Technology

Blockchain technology has the potential to revolutionize various aspects of our lives, offering numerous benefits in terms of transparency, security, efficiency, and decentralization. In this chapter, we will explore how individuals, businesses, and society as a whole can harness the power of blockchain technology to drive positive change and unlock new opportunities.

1. Enhanced Security and Trust

One of the most significant benefits of blockchain technology is enhanced security and trust. Unlike traditional centralized systems, where data is stored in a single location and vulnerable to hacking and manipulation, blockchain uses cryptographic techniques and decentralized networks to ensure the integrity and immutability of data.

As an individual, you can benefit from blockchain's enhanced security by leveraging decentralized applications (dApps) and platforms that utilize blockchain technology. For example, blockchain-based digital wallets offer secure storage for your cryptocurrencies, protecting them from theft and unauthorized access.

2. Improved Transparency and Accountability

Blockchain technology promotes transparency and accountability by providing a tamper-proof and auditable record of transactions. Each transaction recorded on the blockchain is immutable and transparent, allowing individuals to verify the authenticity and integrity of data without relying on intermediaries.

As a consumer, you can benefit from improved transparency and accountability in various industries, such as supply chain management, healthcare, and voting systems. Blockchain-powered supply chain platforms enable you to trace the origins of products, verify their authenticity, and ensure ethical sourcing practices.

3. Empowerment and Financial Inclusion

Blockchain technology has the potential to empower individuals and promote financial inclusion by eliminating barriers to access and enabling peer-to-peer transactions without intermediaries. Through blockchain-based digital identities and payment systems, individuals in underserved communities can access financial services and participate in the global economy.

For example, blockchain-powered microlending platforms allow individuals to borrow and lend funds directly without the need for traditional financial institutions. This enables individuals without access to traditional banking services to obtain credit and invest in their futures.

4. Streamlined Processes and Efficiency Gains

Blockchain technology streamlines processes and drives efficiency gains by eliminating manual paperwork, reducing intermediaries, and automating complex tasks through smart contracts. Smart contracts are self-executing contracts with the terms directly written into code, enabling the automatic execution of agreements without the need for intermediaries.

As a business owner or entrepreneur, you can benefit from blockchain's efficiency gains by integrating blockchain technology into your operations. For example, blockchain-based supply chain management systems can optimize logistics, reduce costs, and enhance traceability and accountability throughout the supply chain.

5. Democratization of Ownership and Control

Blockchain technology facilitates the democratization of ownership and control by enabling decentralized governance models and peer-to-peer collaboration. Decentralized autonomous organizations (DAOs) are entities governed by smart contracts and controlled by their members, allowing for transparent and decentralized decision-making processes.

As a participant in a DAO or decentralized platform, you can benefit from greater ownership and control over the services and products you use. By participating in governance decisions and contributing to the network, you have a say in shaping the future direction of the platform and ensuring that it aligns with your values and interests.

6. Innovation and Entrepreneurship

Blockchain technology fosters innovation and entrepreneurship by providing a fertile ground for experimentation and the development of new business models and applications. The decentralized nature of blockchain enables permissionless innovation, allowing anyone to create and deploy decentralized applications without seeking approval from centralized authorities.

As an innovator or entrepreneur, you can benefit from blockchain's open and inclusive ecosystem by exploring new opportunities and building innovative solutions to address real-world challenges. Whether you are developing decentralized finance (DeFi) platforms, non-fungible token (NFT) marketplaces, or blockchain-based social networks, blockchain technology provides a platform for creativity and innovation.

Blockchain technology offers a myriad of benefits for individuals, businesses, and society as a whole. From enhanced security and transparency to empowerment and innovation, blockchain has the potential to transform industries, disrupt traditional business models, and drive positive change.

By understanding the potential applications and benefits of blockchain technology, you can seize opportunities to leverage blockchain in your personal and professional endeavors. Whether you are seeking to enhance security, streamline processes, promote financial inclusion, or drive innovation, blockchain technology offers a wealth of possibilities to explore and embrace.

7.1. Leveraging Blockchain for Business Innovation

Blockchain technology has emerged as a powerful tool for driving innovation in various industries, offering new ways to streamline processes, enhance security, and create value for businesses. In this section, we will explore how organizations can leverage blockchain technology to drive innovation and gain a competitive edge in the marketplace.

1. Supply Chain Management

Blockchain technology offers significant potential for transforming supply chain management by providing a transparent and immutable record of transactions and events throughout the supply chain. By leveraging blockchain, businesses can enhance visibility, traceability, and accountability across their supply chains, leading to improved efficiency, reduced costs, and enhanced trust among stakeholders.

For example, blockchain-based supply chain platforms enable businesses to track the movement of goods from the point of origin to the final destination in real time, ensuring compliance with regulations, verifying product authenticity, and reducing the risk of counterfeit goods entering the supply chain.

2. Digital Identity Management

Blockchain technology can revolutionize digital identity management by providing individuals with secure and self-sovereign identities that they control and manage. Traditional identity management systems are often fragmented, centralized, and prone to security breaches, leading to privacy concerns and identity theft.

By leveraging blockchain-based identity solutions, businesses can empower individuals to control their data and selectively share it with trusted parties, reducing the risk of data breaches and identity fraud. Blockchain-based digital identities offer a secure and tamper-proof way to verify identities, authenticate users, and streamline identity verification processes.

3. Financial Services

Blockchain technology is reshaping the landscape of financial services by enabling faster, cheaper, and more secure transactions without the need for intermediaries. From cross-border payments to decentralized finance (DeFi) applications, blockchain offers numerous opportunities for innovation in the financial sector.

For example, blockchain-based payment systems enable businesses to conduct cross-border transactions in real time, bypassing traditional banking intermediaries and reducing transaction costs. DeFi platforms leverage smart contracts and decentralized networks to provide financial services such as lending, borrowing, and trading without the need for traditional financial institutions, opening up new avenues for innovation and financial inclusion.

4. Intellectual Property Rights Management

Blockchain technology can revolutionize the management of intellectual property rights by providing a secure and transparent platform for tracking and managing digital assets such as patents, copyrights, and trademarks. Traditional systems for managing intellectual property rights are often cumbersome, time-consuming, and prone to disputes and infringement.

By leveraging blockchain-based solutions, businesses can create immutable records of intellectual property ownership, track the usage and licensing of digital assets, and enforce intellectual property rights more effectively. Blockchain-based systems offer transparent and auditable mechanisms for verifying the authenticity and provenance of digital assets, reducing the risk of piracy and infringement.

5. Healthcare Data Management

Blockchain technology has the potential to revolutionize healthcare data management by providing a secure and interoperable platform for storing, sharing, and accessing patient records and medical information. Traditional healthcare data management systems are often siloed, fragmented, and vulnerable to data breaches and privacy violations.

By leveraging blockchain-based solutions, healthcare organizations can create secure and decentralized repositories of patient data, enabling secure and auditable access to medical records by authorized parties. Blockchain-based systems offer enhanced privacy and security features, such as encryption and access controls, to protect sensitive patient information from unauthorized access and tampering.

Blockchain technology offers immense potential for driving innovation and transforming business processes across various industries. By leveraging blockchain, organizations can enhance transparency, security, and efficiency in supply chain management, digital identity management, financial services, intellectual property rights management, healthcare data management, and many other areas.

To unlock the full potential of blockchain technology, businesses must embrace a mindset of innovation and experimentation, explore new use cases and applications, and collaborate with industry stakeholders and technology partners to drive adoption and create value. By harnessing the power of blockchain for business innovation, organizations can gain a competitive edge in the marketplace and position themselves for success in the digital economy of the future.

7.2. Career Opportunities in Blockchain and Cryptocurrency

The rapid growth and adoption of blockchain and cryptocurrency technologies have created a wealth of career opportunities across various sectors. From technical roles in software development and cryptography to non-technical roles in business development and marketing, there are numerous paths for individuals to pursue a career in the blockchain and cryptocurrency industry. In this section, we will explore some of the exciting career opportunities available in this dynamic and rapidly evolving field.

1. Blockchain Developer

Blockchain developers are responsible for designing, building, and maintaining blockchain-based applications and platforms. They work with programming languages such as Solidity, Java, and Python to develop smart contracts, decentralized applications (dApps), and blockchain protocols. Blockchain developers play a crucial role in driving innovation and building the infrastructure that powers the blockchain ecosystem.

2. Cryptocurrency Trader

Cryptocurrency traders buy, sell, and exchange cryptocurrencies on various trading platforms to profit from market fluctuations. They analyze market trends, monitor price movements, and execute trades based on their assessment of market conditions. Cryptocurrency trading requires a deep understanding of financial markets, technical analysis, and risk management strategies.

3. Blockchain Architect

Blockchain architects design and oversee the implementation of blockchain solutions for businesses and organizations. They work closely with stakeholders to understand their requirements and design scalable, secure, and interoperable blockchain architectures. Blockchain architects are responsible for evaluating different blockchain platforms, selecting the appropriate technology stack, and ensuring that the solution meets the organization's needs.

4. Cryptocurrency Analyst

Cryptocurrency analysts research and analyze market trends, news, and events to provide insights and recommendations to investors and traders. They track cryptocurrency prices, trading volumes, and market sentiment to identify investment opportunities and risks. Cryptocurrency analysts often work for financial institutions, investment firms, or cryptocurrency exchanges.

5. Blockchain Project Manager

Blockchain project managers oversee the planning, execution, and delivery of blockchain projects within organizations. They coordinate cross-functional teams, set project goals and timelines, and ensure that projects are completed on time and within budget. Blockchain project managers need strong leadership, communication, and project management skills to navigate the complexities of implementing blockchain solutions.

6. Cryptocurrency Compliance Officer

Cryptocurrency compliance officers are responsible for ensuring that organizations comply with regulatory requirements and industry standards related to cryptocurrencies and blockchain technology. They develop and implement compliance policies and procedures, conduct risk assessments, and liaise with regulatory authorities to ensure compliance with applicable laws and regulations.

7. Blockchain Consultant

Blockchain consultants advise businesses and organizations on how to leverage blockchain technology to solve business challenges and achieve strategic objectives. They assess the feasibility of blockchain solutions, conduct market research, and develop implementation strategies. Blockchain consultants help clients navigate the complexities of blockchain adoption and drive innovation within their organizations.

8. Cryptocurrency Marketing Specialist

Cryptocurrency marketing specialists develop and execute marketing campaigns to promote cryptocurrencies, blockchain projects, and related products and services. They create content for websites, social media platforms, and other marketing channels to raise awareness, attract users, and drive adoption. Cryptocurrency marketing specialists need a strong understanding of digital marketing techniques and the ability to communicate complex concepts to a diverse audience.

The blockchain and cryptocurrency industry offers a wide range of exciting career opportunities for individuals with diverse skill sets and backgrounds. Whether you are a software developer, financial analyst, project manager, or marketing specialist, there are numerous paths to pursue a rewarding career in this dynamic and rapidly evolving field. By staying informed about industry trends, acquiring relevant skills and certifications, and networking with industry professionals, you can position yourself for success in the fast-growing blockchain and cryptocurrency industry.

7.3. Personal Finance: Using Cryptocurrency for Payments and Savings

Cryptocurrency has emerged as a powerful tool for managing personal finances, offering individuals new ways to make payments, save money, and invest for the future. In this section, we will explore how you can leverage cryptocurrency for payments and savings to enhance your financial well-being and achieve your financial goals.

1. Making Payments with Cryptocurrency

Cryptocurrency offers a convenient and secure alternative to traditional payment methods for making purchases and transactions. Many merchants and online retailers now accept cryptocurrency as a form of payment, allowing you to buy goods and services using your favorite cryptocurrencies.

To make payments with cryptocurrency, you can use a digital wallet that supports the currencies you wish to spend. Simply scan the merchant's QR code or enter their wallet address, specify the amount you want to send, and confirm the transaction. Cryptocurrency transactions are fast, borderless, and secure, making them ideal for online purchases and international transactions.

2. Saving and Investing in Cryptocurrency

Cryptocurrency can also serve as a valuable tool for saving and investing for the future. Many people choose to hold onto their cryptocurrencies as a long-term investment, hoping that their value will increase over time. By investing in cryptocurrencies with strong fundamentals and growth potential, you can potentially earn significant returns on your investment.

Additionally, some cryptocurrencies offer staking and yield farming opportunities, allowing you to earn passive income by locking up your coins in a smart contract or decentralized finance (DeFi) platform. Staking rewards and yield farming incentives can provide a steady stream of income while allowing you to maintain ownership and control of your assets.

3. Diversifying Your Portfolio

Cryptocurrency can play a valuable role in diversifying your investment portfolio and hedging against traditional financial assets such as stocks, bonds, and fiat currencies. Cryptocurrency markets often have a low correlation with traditional markets, meaning that they can provide a valuable source of diversification and risk mitigation.

By allocating a portion of your investment portfolio to cryptocurrency assets, you can potentially reduce overall portfolio volatility and enhance long-term returns. However, it's essential to exercise caution and conduct thorough research before investing in cryptocurrencies, as they can be highly volatile and speculative.

4. Managing Risks and Volatility

While cryptocurrency offers numerous benefits for personal finance, it's essential to manage risks and volatility effectively to protect your investments and financial well-being. Cryptocurrency markets can be highly volatile, with prices fluctuating dramatically in a short period.

To manage risks and volatility, consider diversifying your cryptocurrency holdings across different assets and investment strategies. Additionally, set clear investment goals and risk tolerance levels, and stick to your investment plan regardless of short-term market fluctuations.

5. Staying Informed and Educated

As with any financial instrument, staying informed and educated about cryptocurrency is crucial for making informed decisions and maximizing returns. Keep abreast of industry news, market trends, and regulatory developments that may impact the value and usability of cryptocurrencies.

Take advantage of educational resources such as online courses, webinars, and articles to deepen your understanding of cryptocurrency technology, investment strategies, and security best practices. By staying informed and educated, you can navigate the complex world of cryptocurrency with confidence and make sound financial decisions that align with your goals and risk tolerance.

Cryptocurrency offers exciting opportunities for managing personal finances, from making payments and saving money to investing for the future. By leveraging cryptocurrency for payments and savings, you can enjoy the benefits of fast, secure transactions, potentially earn passive income through staking and yield farming, and diversify your investment portfolio to mitigate risks and enhance returns.

However, it's essential to approach cryptocurrency with caution and diligence, as the market can be highly volatile and speculative. By staying informed, managing risks effectively, and adhering to sound investment principles, you can harness the power of cryptocurrency to achieve your financial goals and build long-term wealth.

7.4. Participating in the Blockchain Community: Education and Networking

Engaging with the blockchain community can be a valuable opportunity to expand your knowledge, build connections, and stay informed about the latest developments in blockchain technology and cryptocurrency. In this section, we will explore how you can participate in the blockchain community through education and networking to enhance your understanding and involvement in this dynamic and rapidly evolving field.

1. Education and Skill Development

One of the first steps to participating in the blockchain community is to invest in your education and skill development. Blockchain technology is complex and multifaceted, encompassing a wide range of concepts, technologies, and applications. By acquiring knowledge and skills in areas such as blockchain fundamentals, cryptography, smart contracts, and decentralized finance (DeFi), you can gain a deeper understanding of blockchain technology and its potential applications.

There are numerous resources available for learning about blockchain, including online courses, tutorials, webinars, and educational platforms. Consider enrolling in blockchain courses offered by reputable institutions and organizations, participating in blockchain certification programs, and joining online communities and forums where you can ask questions, share knowledge, and collaborate with other learners.

2. Networking and Community Engagement

Networking and community engagement are essential aspects of participating in the blockchain community. By connecting with other blockchain enthusiasts, professionals, and experts, you can gain valuable insights, exchange ideas, and build relationships that can help advance your career and personal development.

Attend blockchain conferences, meetups, and workshops in your area to meet like-minded individuals and engage in discussions about the latest trends and innovations in blockchain technology. Join online communities and forums such as Reddit, Telegram, and Discord, where you can connect with blockchain enthusiasts from around the world, participate in discussions, and share your knowledge and experiences.

3. Contributing to Open Source Projects

Contributing to open-source projects is another excellent way to participate in the blockchain community and make a meaningful impact. Many blockchain projects and protocols are open source, meaning that their source code is publicly available and can be freely accessed, modified, and redistributed by anyone.

Consider contributing to open-source blockchain projects by submitting bug fixes, proposing new features, and participating in code reviews and discussions. By contributing to open-source projects, you can gain hands-on experience, build your reputation within the community, and collaborate with other developers and contributors to advance the state of the art in blockchain technology.

4. Sharing Knowledge and Thought Leadership

Sharing your knowledge and thought leadership is a powerful way to contribute to the blockchain community and establish yourself as a trusted authority in your field. Consider writing blog posts, articles, or whitepapers about blockchain-related topics, sharing your insights and experiences through public speaking engagements or webinars, and participating in podcasts or interviews to share your expertise with a wider audience.

By sharing your knowledge and thought leadership, you can help educate and inspire others, foster meaningful discussions, and contribute to the advancement of blockchain technology and its applications. Additionally, sharing your expertise can help raise your profile within the community and create new opportunities for career growth and collaboration.

Participating in the blockchain community through education and networking is a valuable opportunity to expand your knowledge, build connections, and contribute to the advancement of blockchain technology and cryptocurrency. By investing in your education, networking with other enthusiasts, contributing to open-source projects and sharing your knowledge and thought leadership, you can play an active role in shaping the future of blockchain and realizing its full potential to drive positive change and innovation.

7.5. Preparing for the Future: Staying Ahead in a Blockchain-Driven World

As blockchain technology continues to reshape industries and transform the way we live, work, and transact, it's essential to prepare for the future and stay ahead in a blockchain-driven world. In this section, we will explore strategies for staying informed, acquiring relevant skills, and embracing opportunities in the rapidly evolving landscape of blockchain and cryptocurrency.

1. Continuous Learning and Adaptation

Continuous learning and adaptation are critical for staying ahead in a blockchain-driven world. Blockchain technology is constantly evolving, with new developments, innovations, and use cases emerging at a rapid pace. By staying informed about the latest trends, advancements, and regulatory changes in blockchain and cryptocurrency, you can position yourself to adapt to new opportunities and challenges as they arise.

Invest in ongoing education and professional development to acquire and enhance your skills in blockchain technology, cryptography, smart contracts, and decentralized finance (DeFi). Enroll in online courses, attend workshops and webinars, and participate in industry conferences and events to stay up-to-date with the latest developments and best practices in blockchain.

2. Embracing Innovation and Experimentation

Embracing innovation and experimentation is essential for thriving in a blockchain-driven world. Blockchain technology enables new business models, processes, and applications that have the potential to disrupt traditional industries and create new opportunities for growth and innovation. By embracing experimentation and exploring new use cases for blockchain, you can identify innovative solutions to real-world problems and differentiate yourself in the marketplace.

Don't be afraid to experiment with new ideas, technologies, and business models in the blockchain space. Start small, iterate quickly, and learn from both successes and failures. By embracing a culture of innovation and experimentation, you can discover new opportunities, drive value for your organization, and stay ahead of the curve in a rapidly evolving landscape.

3. Building a Strong Network

Building a strong network of peers, mentors, and industry professionals is essential for staying ahead in a blockchain-driven world. Networking allows you to exchange ideas, share knowledge, and collaborate with others who share your passion for blockchain and cryptocurrency. By connecting with like-minded individuals and building relationships within the blockchain community, you can access valuable resources, opportunities, and insights that can help accelerate your career and personal development.

Attend blockchain meetups, conferences, and networking events to meet new people and expand your network. Join online communities and forums where you can engage in discussions, ask questions, and share your expertise with others. By actively participating in the blockchain community, you can build relationships, gain visibility, and create new opportunities for collaboration and growth.

4. Fostering Creativity and Problem-Solving Skills

Fostering creativity and problem-solving skills is essential for staying ahead in a blockchain-driven world. Blockchain technology presents complex challenges and opportunities that require innovative thinking and creative problem-solving abilities. By cultivating a mindset of curiosity, experimentation, and resilience, you can navigate the complexities of blockchain technology and adapt to new opportunities and challenges as they arise.

Practice critical thinking, analytical reasoning, and lateral thinking to approach problems from different perspectives and develop innovative solutions. Collaborate with others, seek feedback, and embrace constructive criticism to continuously improve and refine your ideas and approaches. By fostering creativity and problem-solving skills, you can thrive in a blockchain-driven world and contribute to the advancement of blockchain technology and its applications.

Preparing for the future in a blockchain-driven world requires a commitment to continuous learning, innovation, networking, and problem-solving. By staying informed, embracing innovation, building a strong network, and fostering creativity, you can position yourself to thrive in the rapidly evolving landscape of blockchain and cryptocurrency. Embrace opportunities, adapt to change, and stay curious to unlock new possibilities and create value in the exciting world of blockchain technology.

Conclusion

In this beginner's guide to blockchain technology, we have embarked on a journey to demystify the revolutionary technology behind Bitcoin and cryptocurrency. We've explored the fundamental concepts of blockchain, delved into its transformative impact on the financial world, and uncovered the myriad ways in which individuals, businesses, and society as a whole can benefit from its adoption.

Blockchain technology represents more than just a new way to transact; it embodies a paradigm shift in how we think about trust, transparency, and decentralization. By providing a secure, immutable, and transparent ledger of transactions, blockchain has the potential to revolutionize industries, disrupt traditional business models, and empower individuals with greater control over their financial destinies.

Through the lens of this guide, we've learned how blockchain enables peer-to-peer transactions without the need for intermediaries, how it enhances security and transparency in supply chain management and digital identity management, and how it fosters financial inclusion and innovation through decentralized finance (DeFi) and tokenization.

As we stand on the brink of a blockchain-driven future, the opportunities are boundless for those who dare to embrace the technology and harness its potential. Whether you're a seasoned investor looking to diversify your portfolio, an entrepreneur seeking to revolutionize your industry, or simply a curious individual eager to learn more about the future of finance, blockchain offers a world of possibilities waiting to be explored.

But with great opportunity comes great responsibility. As you navigate the complexities of blockchain technology and cryptocurrency, remember to exercise caution, conduct thorough research, and stay informed about the risks and challenges that accompany this nascent industry.

Above all, remember that blockchain is not just a technology; it's a movement—a global community of innovators, dreamers, and visionaries working together to build a better, more inclusive financial system for the future.

So, as you embark on your journey into the world of blockchain, may you find inspiration, empowerment, and enlightenment along the way. May you seize the opportunities that lie ahead with courage, curiosity, and conviction.

For in the blockchain revolution, the future is not just something to be imagined—it's something to be created. Together, we have the power to shape a future that is more equitable, transparent, and decentralized for generations to come.